MOORLAND DOCTOR

R. W. S. BISHOP

Moorland Doctor

GEORGE MANN • MAIDSTONE

R.W.S. Bishop

MOORLAND DOCTOR

First published in the United Kingdom by
John Murray, May 1922
under the title of
My Moorland Patients

First published under the title
Moorland Doctor
by George Mann 1973

This edition first published 1989

ISBN 0 7041 0242 0

Printed and bound in Great Britain
by WBC Print Ltd., Bristol

and published by
George Mann of Maidstone
in
England's County of Kent

Preface — 1920

THESE pages are my response to the insistent
demand of friends that I would place on per-
manent record tales I have told them after dinner
or over the smoking-room fire of the moorland
folk with whose ways and speech my many years
of practice on the Yorkshire moors have made
me familiar.

Although the period of time covered concludes
so recently as the outbreak of the Great War, these
narratives may not be without value. Life and
character on the moorlands is rapidly changing.
With the coming of the motor car and cycle, the
charm and seclusion of remote England has nearly
departed. No far off moorland lane is now free
from their intrusion, and it is fortunate that they
cannot yet jump the stone walls and hedges, so
that the footpaths are still left to us. What it
will be like when the air is thick with flying
machines, I will not attempt to imagine.

With so many intruders, the old kindly
hospitality is rapidly vanishing. Compulsory
standard education is responsible for the disappearance of countless old words and distinc-
tions of dialect. Old customs and usages have
been dropped. Superstition is practically dead.
Those uplands, so suitable for stock-breeding and

rearing, are now being given over to dairying. The stock-markets, which are everywhere, have limited the frequency and fierceness of the old Yorkshire bargainings.

My days are now, alas, filled with sadness and suffering, but the memory of past happy years, when I received the love and affection of so many of my moorland patients, is a compensation that is priceless.

Contents

CONTENTS

Moorland Doctor

CHAPTER I

THE MOORS AND THE MOORLANDERS: MY PATIENTS

NEARLY the whole of my professional life as a doctor has been spent on the Peak of Derbyshire, and the high moorlands of South and North-West Yorkshire. It has, naturally, been a hard and exacting one, and full of drawbacks and difficulties. The people were often ignorant and prejudiced, the distances were great, the roads, specially in my younger days, were bad, and the climate was severe for many months in the year. Men of like education and position, with whom I could associate on anything like intimate terms, were few, and often far off.

The hum and bustle of modern existence were almost beyond the horizon. Amusements in the current sense were unknown.

On the other hand it was God's own country, scarce touched by man's defiling hand. The pages of the great book of Nature were always invitingly open, and there were ample opportunities for sport of every kind.

The people, on the whole, were most kind and hospitable. Their folk-lore, habits, and language were a source of perpetual interest and study, and, if the conditions were trying, it was a healthy land.

The air was always tonic and conducive to energy, and even on the hottest days of midsummer we were rarely without a refreshing breeze.

A country doctor's patients are all more or less stationary, and in this respect he has a very great advantage over his brother practitioner in the towns, who has to deal with a continually moving procession. As time went on I got to know quite well the individual character and mentality of all my patients, as well as their physical constitution. This knowledge saved a great deal of time, and was very helpful. I knew beforehand whom to coax, flatter, or coerce. Of all the problems the human problem is far away the most difficult to solve and the most interesting.

I remember one day a friend remarking to me, "You look rather worried, Doctor." "Not a little," was my reply. "I have just seen two women living next door to each other; one I cannot persuade to go to bed, the other I cannot persuade to get out of bed."

It is said that the parson knows a man at his best, the lawyer knows him at his worst, but that only the doctor knows him as he really is. This is true. When man is sick and racked with bodily or mental pain, he recognises his frailty; all his artificiality and veneer depart for the while, and his true character is revealed. The country doctor who knows how to make use of this opportunity and tries to live up to the highest ideals of his profession, is a privileged being, wielding great power and bearing a great responsibility in his little kingdom. He sees Jack and Jill, whom he brought into the world, grow up and develop. He becomes the confidential friend of the family, the trusted adviser in important events, and the depositary of sacred secrets. His life is so rich in human problems that he can never be dull.

My neighbours perhaps differed more from one another in character, personality, and habits than human beings ordinarily do. Such differences were conspicuous in a sparsely populated country, and became exaggerated by isolation.

Dwellers in towns, like stones in the pot-hole of a river-bed, have all their edges and peculiarities rounded off.

In the country, on the other hand, there is so much elbow-room for everybody that individual eccentricities are accentuated, and the edges of character become sharp and rugged. Moreover, in the country, everybody knows everything about everybody and seeks to know more. Curiosity is rampant. It is said that country people will even look down the chimney to see what their neighbours are having for breakfast. An unused chimney sending forth for the nonce its volume of smoke advertises to the country-side that something unusual is on foot. "Another chimbley smoking at Trotter's this morn." "What's up? Onnyways t'bairn isn't looked for yet awhile. Must be his sister fra Lunnon, or yon painting chap is there ageean." Country curiosity is insatiable. Paul Prys abound. Eavesdropping is no disgrace. One salutes the passer-by in the dark, purely in order to recognise the voice and guess what his business may be. The village postman in those days would read all the correspondence he could, and then retail it for his neighbours' benefit. One local postman I knew made a sad blunder. After steaming two letters open he put the letters into the wrong envelopes, and of course there was trouble, which sent him back to cobbling and bitter reflections.

I knew of an incident where, to satisfy an extreme curiosity, a ladder was noiselessly ascended to the window of a particular bedroom. A statement was made to me once in confidence, so extraordinary and unbelievable, that I refused to credit it. I said, "I don't believe a word of it. It's all rubbish." "It may be rubbish," was the reply, "but Ah see'd it all wi' me 'ain ees." Then I realised what it meant to have seen with his own eyes, and hurried away in disgust. It was a case of incest.

I give the following as an example of country curiosity. One of my patients was a widow, who with a son and grandson farmed a small holding some five or six miles away. She was a toothless old lady, and the only meal of the day she really fancied was a late supper to which she "reached with a long arm," consuming often most indigestible foods, with the natural result that, in the small hours of the morning, she frequently had attacks of severe indigestion. So painful were these attacks, which she called the "spavins," that she thought of course she was going to die at once, and very urgent messages would be sent demanding my immediate attendance.

These hasty summonses came so constantly and the payment of her bill so rarely, that I became chary of responding, and arranged with my wife that she should answer the calls through the bedroom window. Early one winter's morning it was the old story. "Please tell the Doctor to come to Mrs Lonsdale, she's got t'spavins despert bad, and weeant live till morning, unless summat's deän right sharp," was the message two men brought. My wife answered, "The Doctor has gone to Mardale, and I will send him along as soon as he returns." Then she said "good-night" and closed the window, and we went off to sleep again. Now I must explain that Mardale was a distant dale, with many farms, and it was one undertaking to arrive there and another to return therefrom. But within half an hour we were again roused from our slumbers, with a much more peremptory message. "Tell the Doctor to come at once to Mrs Lonsdale. He hasn't gone to Mardale, and is in t'hoos. He can't gan to Mardale widout 'osses." These curious prying fellows had first listened at the locked stable door, then had inspected the coach-house, and finally examined the roadway.

Environment makes the moorsiders hardy, cautious, thrifty, stoical, and self-reliant. On the other hand, they are thereby rendered hard, suspicious, taciturn, quarrelsome, and implacable. When a man is his own chief companion, this solitude makes for strength of mind and happiness so long as all is well within, but should it be otherwise then it makes for the worst. If he drinks, he soon drinks heavily, mental strain or worry develops into madness. Again sparseness of population leads to the practice of endogamy. The frequent intermarrying of cousins was the cause of a great deal of insanity, a subject which I discuss elsewhere, and had a deteriorating effect on the physique of the moorland people. They were by no means a level lot. Some were magnificent stalwart fellows, almost perfect in form and build, but many were only of average height, slightly built or slender, though all were tough and wiry. When I first went to the moorlands the older people had excellent teeth. Some veterans have almost perfect sets; but it was not so with the younger ones. The teeth seemed to go bad in a single generation. This I attribute entirely to the soft, pappy, starch foods and the modern, ultra-white, fine bread, which cause fermentation in the mouth and give the teeth no work to do. They often spoke to me of the rough oat and barley meal, which was the staple food of their forefathers.

Man is a sociable animal, and this social instinct has been the main factor in the civilisation of the world. Civilisation in turn makes men still more sociable. Yet these moorland dwellers loved intensely their lives of solitude, and would not have exchanged them for any other. The "homing" instinct was strong. Those who did venture into the larger world to seek their fortunes invariably returned whether successful or unsuccessful. Many of my patients never wandered much farther than the neighbouring markets or fairs. Some of the stay-at-home housewives had not even been to the local market for a period of twenty or thirty years, or even longer.

Then there were some of those exceptional beings who had never been in a train. One of these, a farmer, I must describe. He lived in the last house of a ghyll, where a syndicate of jovial sportsmen, who had taken the grouse shooting of the adjacent moors, always lunched. To them his terse, quaint talk was a constant source of interest and amusement. He was a veritable moorland philosopher, with his head as full of wit and wisdom as an egg is full of meat. Nothing would satisfy these good sportsmen but that this rare old moor bird must take his first railway journey into the big world under their auspices. After some consideration he somewhat reluctantly consented. Arrangements for his comfort and enjoyment were liberally made. He travelled first-class one Saturday morning to Leeds, in the company of the head keeper. He had a recherché lunch and dinner at the Queen's Hotel, took a long drive to see the principal buildings and streets, and went finally to a music-hall performance. Naturally he was very "mafted and moidered" with such a sudden plunge into city dissipation, and only too thankful to return safe and sound to his moorland eyrie.

Another farmer whom I knew was in the Yorkshire Yeomanry, and being a smart soldier and good rider was a great favourite with his landlord, the noble lord who commanded the regiment. During the annual training at York, in those days there was always an Easter pantomime. One performance was held under the patronage of the colonel and officers of the regiment. A few days afterwards the noble colonel stopped in the street this man, Caygill, with several other privates who were all his tenants, asking, "How did you enjoy the ballet, Caygill, the other night?" Caygill stared in bewilderment, not understanding. "How did you enjoy the ballet, Caygill?" he repeated. A companion whispered something to Caygill, who now understood and answered very promptly, "If 'tis leg and thigh, ye mean, my Lord, whya I saw mair than eneagh to last me my lifetime."

I shall never forget the deep impression made on my mind by the case of a certain sheep farmer, who was dying by inches from a painful cancer. He had never married, and his only companion, his housekeeper, was a grim, silent old woman, with apparently not a particle of human love or sympathy in her composition. He never read, and there he lay in that lonely and remote farmhouse, always in discomfort or pain, with no one to love, or be loved by, for nearly two long years, waiting without a murmur and with most stoical resignation for the order of release. Such a picture of a lonely heart touches the depth of human pathos. In old age love is as necessary as in childhood.

I one day asked a moorsider how he spent his hours of leisure, and in reply he said, "Ah sits and smokes and thinks, sometimes Ah sits an thinks, and sometimes Ah just sits."

These folk, though having constantly before their eyes scenes of great beauty, perpetually renovated by the interchange of shadow and sunlight, storm and calm, are yet curiously indifferent to or unconscious of all this natural beauty. I cannot say I ever remember one of them drawing my attention to it as a matter of pleasure and delight, though they were proud of their powers of long sight. They could distinguish objects on the horizon which were quite invisible to me, and I could thoroughly appreciate the immense advantage the Boer marksmen had over our men on the veld.

To me in my restless journeyings, the daily panorama of impressive and often entrancing beauty was a continual feast and never - failing joy. It was the clerk of the weather of course who so considerately varied the colouring or altered the perspective for me. Sometimes he was too erratic and capricious for my comfort, but I only really grumbled when he turned on the mists or fogs, or when the deep snows were melting. The most wonderful moments I have ever lived in life have been on those distant moorland hills in the earliest hours from dawn, on a midsummer morning. Then only Nature is to be seen in her freshest beauty, her most exquisite purity.

Even in the more cultivated mind familiarity breeds indifference.

I once asked a country parson, who was retiring after many years' work, and had lived in a most picturesquely and romantically situated moorland vicarage, if he was not loth to leave it for the town to which he was going. He replied that he had lived on scenery nearly forty years, and had had more than enough of it. He longed now for the scenery of human faces. A Yorkshire man who had just paid his first visit to Switzerland was asked on his return for his opinion of that land of mountains. "I reckoned nowt tae it. I could see nowt for t'bloomin' hills."

A moorland clergyman once declined an invitation of his bishop to his palace for a series of "quiet days" by replying that all his days were quiet, but that he would very gladly come if his lordship would kindly arrange for a little earthquake or cataclysm of some sort.

The element of distance of course played an important part in my life. The very long journeys I daily took on my rounds were exceedingly trying, especially in my early days. Before the Local District Councils Act was passed for their improvement, "bad" does not describe the condition of the roads. Many of them were damnable. A certain distant township could be approached by three diverse ways, all equally long and equally bad, and I remember how each time full of hope I would choose a different one, only to regret that I had not taken another. So very bad was one main road that I was compelled to report it to the chief constable. I called on him personally, asking him not to give me away. He was very nice about it, and said by way of a joke, that I evidently wanted him to ride over it and have a big fall so that I might have the pleasure of setting his broken limb. Ten days afterwards I met an army of farmers with carts, looking dreadfully angry and uttering fierce threats against some unknown busybody.

I one day asked a moorsider, or a "moor pout," as these people call themselves, hurrying along the moorland road, how his wife and daughter, whom I was attending, were. Without troubling to stop, he kept on at the same pace answering my questions over his shoulder in what I thought a very rude and surly fashion. A few days later

I tackled him about it. His explanation was very simple. He was sexton of the moorland church, and it was his task to keep the clock in order. But he had no watch. He used to walk the eight miles over the moors to the moorland town every week to make his family purchases, and, when ready to return, would note the correct time of day by the post-office clock. From long experience he knew almost to a minute how long it would take him, going at a fixed pace, to reach home. The clocks of the dale were then set by this scientific and accurate method. They were notoriously correct.

In one historic and long-continued snowstorm it was so many days before I reached the house, where I had been engaged for a confinement, that it was reported up and down dale that my services were then bespoken for the next one. They were such a hardy race, that nearly half my babies were happily born before my arrival. This obviated the long waiting which was necessary in other cases.

A newcomer, a doctor, and successor to one who had died, was hours late for a confinement, and by mistake went to the house of an old maid of the same name as his patient. He rushed into the house with his black bag, exclaiming to the astonished lady, "I hope I am in time."

A rather good story is told of a stranger journeying to a far distant dale in Yorkshire. On arrival at the railway terminus he proceeded to engage a seat in a conveyance plying to his destination. Asked if he required a first-, second-, or third-class ticket, he took a first-class, though not a little mystified by the request. This mystification became annoyance when at the appointed time all crowded into the convey-ance without any distinction of class. He naturally thought he had been "had." However, after a five-mile run on the level, the driver pulled up at the foot of a tremendously long steep hill. "First-class passengers," he directed, "sit still, second-class passengers get out and walk, third-class passengers shove up behind."

Although my moorland friends used to say that third-class riding was better than first-class walking, some of the happiest hours of my life have been spent in walking to the far off moor-land farms, straight across country, over walls and ditches. It was a land of footpaths, many of them made by the feet of the children from the scattered farms, in their daily pilgrimage to and from the moorland school.

The farmers used to drive their horses at top speed headlong down the steepest and roughest roads, covered with loose, rolling stones, with here and there exposed rock or beds of sand. At first I thought it a most reckless, dare-devil fashion, but I found afterwards that it was much the safest and surest way. If accidents did un-fortunately sometimes occur, it was not the fault of their good Galloways or of their driving, but of their rotten old gear. I never had nerve to imitate them, but my man, a real high-sider, knew the game quite well.

I remember being fetched by a farmer in his gig one perfect midsummer morning, to his far distant farmhouse, for a confinement. He was terribly anxious, and we simply flew down several long steep hills at breakneck pace. I have never had such an experience, except when some of my horses have run away. Fortunately the harness held and nothing happened. I was hours before time, and have often remembered the delightfully happy day I spent getting an insight into the life of a large moorland sheep-farm, as I wandered with the farmer after his sheep.

The first steam-roller which came to the moorlands caused much excitement and wonder among the moormen. Crowds gathered to watch it at work. One big fellow became so excited that he had a bad fit and was carried to a moorland inn, where he died six weeks afterwards. The steam-roller was condemned of course at first as a useless expense, but what an incalculable boon and comfort it was. Moorland roads in hot summer weather become exceptionally dry, and before the day of the roller loose stones were everywhere. Even behind the safest of horses there was always anxiety.

One of the greatest difficulties of a doctor's life in a remote unopposed country practice, is the inaccessibility of his nearest medical neighbours. It is the unexpected which always happens. Sudden and quite unforeseen emergencies arise, and when human life is in peril, moments are precious. There must be no delay, no shirking or running away, if one would have that priceless possession, that "music at midnight," a clear conscience.

I know only too well what it means to be miles away from home, in the middle of the night, perhaps wet through and shivering with cold, face to face with one of these great events, only a tallow dip for light, and only one's groom or some handy farmer's wife to hold the ether apparatus. How one longs for two pair of hands, instead of the single pair provided by nature. I must give all praise and credit to the moorland women, that at such crises they exhibited more nerve and resource than the men. I remember one case in particular, during a big snowstorm, when outside help was impossible. Four big strong men one after another took charge of the ether apparatus, only to relinquish it almost immediately in a half-fainting condition, till an active, quick-witted, plucky farmer's wife took hold, and stood firm and fast to the end.

On these exposed moorlands weather was an important factor, and in course of time I became very weather-wise. One farmer described the climate as "nine months' winter and three months' caud weather." The west winds in spring often blew continuously for weeks, and were frequently accompanied by rain, and there were the bitter east winds, the March "Higs." The higher the altitude, of course, the greater the rainfall. Yet at the highest altitudes I have experienced, in mid-winter, heat and brilliant sunshine, when the rolling valleys below were wrapped in a mantle of mist or fog. It was interesting to notice the incidence of thunderstorms, and how the configuration of the hills constantly regulated their track. One farmhouse, now in consequence deserted and in ruins, standing at the edge of a deep ghyll, was struck three times by lightning, once, it was said, when a honeymoon couple were occupying it. In another ghyll on the same spot a horse was killed one year, and the next year in two storms a man on each occasion was struck and severely injured. In another storm I saw the chimney-stacks at either end of an exposed farmhouse struck by successive flashes. On wide, exposed tablelands it was marvellous that there were not more accidents. Often when I was driving across them the lightning seemed to play all round my horse and cart.

My weather wisdom was instinctive rather than constructive, and in course of time I found myself astonishingly correct in reading the omens of the sky. Such wisdom comes naturally to those who are observant and live out of doors. In accord with an old saying, some of the dullest witted moorlanders were numbered among the wisest and most reliable of the weather prophets. The almost constant mist in evidence on the most distant hills is a constant problem and often most difficult to interpret. When the barometer rises very slowly and steadily, this mist on the hills is a sure sign of a spell of dry weather, but if the movement of the barometer is at all erratic it invariably foretells more rain. On the other hand, mornings when the atmosphere is preternaturally clear are often followed by stormy and unsettled weather.

It is scarcely possible adequately to describe a fascinatingly wonderful transformation scene I once witnessed. My man and I were driving over a high tableland to an important burying when the mist or "roke" was so dense that we could scarcely see ten yards from the dogcart.

I had just remarked to him how unfortunate the conditions were for the funeral, when the gentlest of breezes came.   It was so gentle as to be scarcely perceptible.   As if by magic hand the curtains of mist were lifted and moved aside, and, "like the baseless fabric of a vision," almost instantly dissolved.   In the space of only five minutes by my watch I could see the outlines of hills quite twenty miles away.

I recall an even more remarkable instance.   A friend and I drove to a distant moorland vicarage one winter's night in a dense roke.   Such an expedition under such circumstances would to the majority of people have been an impossibility, but in regard to weather no such word exists in moorland vocabularies.   After four miles of the slowest going we stabled the horse at a farmhouse previous to a difficult walk of a mile up and down the braes of a very steep ghyll.   During the five minutes we were engaged in making the mare comfortable, the mist had dissolved so quickly that every star in the firmament was revealed to us to the farthest horizon.   I took back the carriage lamp I had taken to light the way, but required it badly three hours afterwards, when after leaving the hospitable vicarage we found the black pall of mist had returned and was if possible more dense than before.

One must distinguish between moor rokes and fogs, because by the latter is implied a mixture of the roke with town smoke.   How very real this mixture is can be seen by the sooty deposit on the whitest and purest of the moorland snow miles distant from the town after only a few hours of the fog.

Although I had almost second sight in the dark, and have been gifted with an unusually big bump of locality, I have several times been hopelessly lost in a moorland roke. It is quite possible by constant practice to pick up on the darkest night a fairly marked footpath, provided one is alone, and there is not that fatal hindrance, a bright light on the horizon in front. The contiguity of a wall or fence can be appreciated even a couple of yards away. A bull reclining on the footpath is a decidedly uncomfortable distraction. When a farmer once twitted an assistant I had on his carrying a lantern at night, he replied with much asperity, "I haven't cat's eyes like the Doctor."

One night I was summoned to a patient who resided many miles away over the moors. There were two ways to the place, one more devious by moorland road the whole way, and the other by high road for five miles with a little over two miles walk by moorland footpath. I chose the latter. Although there was some moonlight there was a slight roke, which as we gradually ascended became slowly denser. Under such circumstances we invariably drove without lamps risking all fines. The old mare, an experienced roadster, if given her head, instinctively kept the road.

Arriving at the moorland footpath I sent my man home with the dog-cart, and set off on my way with a small hand lantern in case of emergency. The proceeding was by no means free from risk, because on the right were many acres of bog, and on the left a ravine with steep crags, a fall down which would have been instantly fatal. The footpath though rarely used was not ill-defined till it crossed about a quarter of a mile away diagonally a line of grouse butts, where it became very indistinct owing to the heather having been well burnt round about. I knew the path quite well, and carried in my head the exact line and contour of the butts, and the exact angle of crossing. On this occasion I must have wandered from the path just before I reached the butts. The problem was to pick up the path on the other side, whence the way would be comparatively easy, and it could only be done by counting the butts from the extreme right. There was the even greater difficulty that in trying to follow them I might lose them altogether as the roke was now thicker than ever, and this is what eventually happened. Using the greatest caution, I had as I thought accounted for two butts when I lost them altogether. I lit the lantern, but that only made matters worse. I tried to find the shorter heather, but I had wandered even from that too. I was hopelessly lost, and the only thing to be done, as it was perishingly cold, was to keep moving very very slowly on, if possible to higher ground. When after what seemed an eternity daylight dawned four hours afterwards, I found I had wandered fortunately well away from the bog to higher ground close to the road, and I knew where I was.

How the right arm pulls on such an occasion the following incident shows. Under similar circumstances I was obliged to cross a wide moorland allotment of many acres, across which were three footpaths, with all of which I was familiar. I got through an "owergaat" (stone stile), and after half an hour's slow going came to another owergaat which I could not remember ever to have seen before and which I stared at in bewilderment. It was unrecognisable, and my wonder was so great that I even took the trouble to pinch myself to see if I was quite awake. Satisfied on this point, I thought perhaps by getting over the stile I might come nearer to a solution of its identity and my whereabouts, and when I did so found to my surprise that it was the same stile I had got over half an hour previously. So I essayed again, and at the end of twenty minutes found myself back again at this fatally magnetic "owergaat." The only course to save my reason was to take another footpath, which though a most inconvenient detour eventually brought me home.

One gloomy winter's afternoon just before dark, when the moorlands were lying deep in snow, I remarked to a farmer whose house I was just leaving that I intended taking a short cut to a neighbouring but a very inaccessible farm, from which in another direction there was an easy way home. Till then this comparatively wild and desolate part of the country was almost unknown to me, necessitating frequent reference to the map. Beyond staring rather fixedly at me for a few seconds, the farmer, who was a stolid fellow, merely replied, "Ye mun tak care, Doctor." His wife described to me afterwards that during the whole of the following evening he seemed pre-occupied and worried, till at nine o'clock, he suddenly lit a stable lantern, remarking that he could "bahd it ner langer" (bide it no longer). Pressed for an explanation, he said that he was afraid I might have fallen down a steep unprotected precipice, which I must have passed on my way, and about which he had omitted to warn me.   He followed my footsteps through the snow, and was much relieved to find that I had safely passed it, though within a margin of only about eight inches. When I saw for the first time by daylight what I had safely avoided, I don't wonder he was perturbed in mind.

Do pigs really see the wind as the old country gaffers affirm, or is the following occurrence merely a coincidence? While walking the horse up a steep road past a wayside farmhouse on the afternoon of a perfect spring day, my groom and I beheld a big porker leave its precincts and proceed with most business-like mien to a sugar-loaf hill in the adjacent field, which was quite a conspicuous landmark. Arrived at the summit he surveyed for a few minutes the wide landscape unfolded, turning his head alternately from side to side in ludicrously human-like deliberation. If pigs' eyes can see as far as human eyes, this porker's must have taken in a view of at least thirty-five miles. Suddenly he turned his head homewards and bolted as fast as his legs could carry him, snorting horribly all the while. "What an extraordinary performance," I remarked to my Yorkshire man. "Nowt o't soart," he answered. "It's seein' t'wind, and we sall have some varra mucky weather." My man was surprised and not a little contemptuous to find me ignorant of so well known a fact of natural history. The same night there was a terrific gale. "Ah tauld yer seea," was his triumphant comment next morning.

The snowstorms were, however, my greatest

bugbear and trial.   The moorland roads and tracks were often hopelessly blocked by snow-drifts for weeks.   It was sometimes days before I could reach my patients.   First I would abandon my cart, then my horse, and finally perhaps, after wading nearly waist deep for some distance, would be compelled to relinquish the struggle.   Once when attending the pretty old lady of the moor, I was obliged to go to bed for four hours till I had recovered from my strenuous toil.

The nine weeks' storm of 1895 was of course the record storm.   Till the great thaw came, the moorlands were covered deep with snow, which, owing to continuous frost and slight mid-day thaws, became firmly frozen over on the surface, so that one could walk without difficulty straight across country over the buried stone walls.   Many houses were deep in drifts, and in one homestead the household were roused from their slumbers by hearing the sheep on the roof.   The roads were continually opened by an army of farmers, only to be blocked again by recurring blizzards.   The moorland sheep were brought to the lowlands, where also flocked the moorcock and all moor-land birds.

In a remote ghyll lived a farmer and his house-keeper.   She had been his housekeeper and mistress for twenty-three years.   Often and often the moor-land parson had implored him to marry her and make her an honest woman.   At last he consented, and the "spurrings" were read out for the first time on the Sunday before the great storm.   Un-fortunately the woman was taken seriously ill a few days afterwards. I made repeated journeys when I could to the distant farmhouse, because I was more than anxious under the circumstances to save her life. The neighbouring farmers were most sympathetic in keeping a way open for me. But alas! it was willed otherwise and our efforts were vain. To the deep sorrow of the whole ghyll she passed gently away. She was buried in her bridal dress, and her bier was dragged by hand over the great snowdrifts to the moorland church.

Thrift was a natural concomitant of an existence where there were no shops to tempt, or amusements to attract. There was a saying that when sixpence went over the local bridge it never returned.

One very thrifty wife used to give her husband, a huge man, threepence for the refreshment of his big body, when he set off on the fourteen miles' task of fetching a rare load of coals, and more often than not he would return the threepence, and look for the word of praise she would always bestow.

Some were more than thrifty, they were mean and miserly, and almost too miserable to live. They were by long habit real misers, and the grasping and hoarding were the main object of life and the only source of happiness. The predominant partner in meanness was invariably the woman. I doubt if it is really possible for a man to be as mean as a woman can be. I used to look at these crabby, thin, industrious, and mean "scrats," and wonder if ever they had had feelings of love, romance, or sympathy within their being.

My wife and I were staying at a moorland

farmhouse during the war, and owing to the shortage of labour she had gone one day into the potato field to assist in the picking. This naturally pleased the farmer immensely. The same evening I overheard a conversation between my wife and the farmer's wife. "Aye," said the latter, "Reuben war pleased wi' ye in t'tatie field to-day. He are takken wi' ye, I can tell ye, right takken." Then after a long pause and a deep sigh, she added, "I wish he war harf as takken wi' me." Probably it was entirely her own fault that poor Reuben had ceased to be "takken" with her.

What autocratic power some little shrill-voiced "scauds" seem to wield over their big husbands. I have seen a big six-foot-three policeman, and an ex-soldier, humbly take off his shoes at his wife's bidding, and walk gingerly over the newly swept and garnished kitchen floor.

I knew a head gamekeeper who was a strong, powerful man, and a terror to poachers and evil-doers, and whose second wife had quarrelled with his nearest relation, his only sister, forbidding him to have any dealings with her. He was obliged to get three parts drunk before ever he ventured to pay her a visit at her moorland farm. Once she was dreadfully ill and nearly died. It was a long time before I could understand his strange conduct in being always so drunk while his sister's life was in danger. In this drunken state he would often come to inquire about her, or fetch her medicine, and was dreadfully quarrelsome and offensive. All this to-do and fuss because he was afraid of his angelic-looking, baby-faced wife.

The following is an extreme example of thrift and greediness.   The vicar of one moorland parish, who had a fancy for rare breeds of poultry, one day unexpectedly purchased a pen of birds of quite a new variety, but had no run ready for them. He approached a neighbouring farmer who had an isolated farm building, asking him to take charge of them for a few weeks till accommodation was ready, and to keep the eggs in return for the keep. As they were all laying, it was a profitable bargain for the farmer, and he readily consented.   A few days afterwards the vicar went for a sitting of eggs, and, knowing his man, offered him the market price of a shilling per sitting.   "Nay, Nay, Nay," said the farmer.   "Them's a particular soart, and Ah's sellin' 'em at two-and-sixpence a sitting," and he declined to let the vicar have the sitting at a lower rate.

They would never pay a doctor for his time or advice under any circumstances, though they were quite willing to pay for the bottle and mileage. They never paid their bills till they were obliged, and then always expected something back.   They were always anxious of course that everything possible should be done in illness, when it was absolutely necessary, but not a whit beyond that. "Mi missus is deean," they would say; "she's wore out, so if you can't dea her any mair good, whya if ye please deeant come any mair."   Three-quarters of the way to a farmhouse I was stopped by the husband of the patient, "Ye moant gan onny mairs now, ye've put her to rights," he said. "What about a bottle of tonic?" I suggested. "Nay, Nay, mi missus an' I we've considered t'matter weel ower, and we're not in favour of another bottle. Ah tell ye we're not favourable." Of course the bottle of medicine, or "stuff," as it is called in Yorkshire, was the outward and only visible cause of cure in their eyes, and the more "meat and drink" about it, with perhaps in addition a taste of "summat warmin'," the better.

One old farmer having come to the conclusion that medicine was by far the most expensive liquor that ever came into his house, invariably finished off all the remnants, with great gusto and satisfaction. As for gargles I never prescribed them for Yorkshire farmers, because the greedy fellows invariably swallowed them. All liquor that goes into a Yorkshireman's mouth, by a natural law must go down his "throttle" instantly.

A stranger on a walking tour called at a Yorkshire moorland inn for a refreshing drink. The only other occupant of the bar was a cattle drover, and in a high good humour he asked the latter if he would have a glass of ale. "Aye, thankee," was the reply, and he immediately swallowed the glassful which had been drawn for him in one "let down." "Will you have another?" asked the kindly stranger. "Thankee ageean," responded the drover, and as promptly swallowed the second glass at one gulp. "Have a third?" offered the stranger, in deep admiration. The third glassful was again promptly "necked" at one asking. Quoth the stranger, "You must be very thirsty." "Noa, Noa," protested the drover. "Yeah seea," very confidentially, "yance Ah had yan knocked ower." "Yan would rather see the Church Broach

(Steeple) fall, than a glass of good liquor be spilt," is quite an old Yorkshire saying.

A Yorkshire farmer called on horseback at a Yorkshire inn for a glass of gin and "watter." After one critical drink he questioned the landlord, "Ah say, did ye put t'gin in fust, or t'watter?" "The gin first of course," was the reply. "Aye, I sall come at it i'noo," was the oracular comment.

A moorland sheep farmer being critically ill, it was decided, on the urgent recommendation of the doctor in attendance to call in from the nearest town a "Physicianer" or "Doctor of advoice," as consultants are often called on the moorland. When the great man had seen the patient and pronounced his verdict, he was asked by the thrifty, if not miserly, wife to name his charge. "My fee will be ten guineas," said the doctor. "Ten fiddlesticks," answered the wife. "Ye surely woant charge all that." "That is my lowest fee," replied the doctor. After giving the latter a very big piece of her mind on the enormity of his fee, she very reluctantly paid the ten guineas. The consultant, no doubt a little influenced by her tirade, kindly offered to come again for half the fee should his services be required further. After his departure the old woman thus delivered herself to the sufferer. "Nae then, he's takken ten pund ten wi' him, and if he comes agean it'll be five pund five. It's a seet o' good brass, bud if I war ye, Ah'd mannish ter dea widout him an' his fangle-ments and die like a Briton."

In like manner one of my farming friends was very graphically describing to another how after a long illness he had paid me a bill of £60, and that on my recommendation he had afterwards drunk £30 worth of good port, before he was fully restored to health. The other remarked very solemnly, "It war a seet o' good brass. Ah knaws what Ah'd a deean. Ah'd a deead sooner."

Another example of meanness. At the weekly market I once asked a moorsider for a lift home, which he cordially agreed to. These people as a rule were only too ready to give a lift on the way to anyone, and no doubt regarded it as some variation of hospitality. Judge of my surprise when thanking him at the end of the journey he remarked, "Noo, we'll call oursens straight ower they twa bottles of stuff Ah got on yer t'other day." I declined to agree to this mean bargain and we came to high words over it. "Never," I said, "ask me for any more stuff." "Never," retorted he, "ask me for any mair lifts." He got the better of me, because I did not report him to the Revenue Authorities, which I felt very much inclined to do.

At the moorland sidings or funerals as an almost universal rule no expense was spared or grudged, even by the most miserly and thrifty. My astonishment was all the greater when in one moorland churchyard I found that several families had "paired" for gravestones, one family using one face and the other the reverse.

During a bad plague of influenza I was attending an old couple in a far-off dale who were both seriously ill. The old man was reported to be fabulously rich. The wealth of any-one rather more fortunate than themselves was

invariably exaggerated by envious moorside neighbours. "He fair stinks o' brass—he's thousands
out at interest—he don't know what he is worth,"
are samples of the usual comment. It is a fact
that this man was well off, and had easily the
cheapest farm in the dale, but so terrified was he
of the rent being raised that he invariably paid
it by instalments, to the secret amusement of
the agent and his clerk. At each farce he used
to say, "I've mannished to bring ee twenty
pund, all I can scrape together these varra
bad times."

But what true loyalty these moorland folk
gave to their old doctors, even when, as sometimes happened, they had by constant neglect,
incapacity, or drunkenness, long forfeited any
claim to it. It was amazing what they would put
up with, and how long-suffering they were.

The greatest demonstration of genuine grief
and emotion by a general body of mourners I ever
witnessed was at the funeral of an old moorland
doctor who had once had a big practice and
reputation, but had nearly ruined it by drink
and incapacity.

I shall never forget a grim, hard moorsider
telling me how at last he had been compelled to
part with this old doctor of many years' service
and friendship. He evidently had felt the parting
terribly. These stoical men rarely showed any
sign of agitation, but there was a suspicious
moisture in his eyes, and a rapid contortion of
his rugged, weather-beaten features when he said,
"Ah tell ee it war warse than having mi ee tooth
drawn. Ah think I would rather have shutten

t'aud dog." Could he possibly have expressed himself more feelingly? A sheep farmer loves his dog more deeply than anything on earth. To me there was no sight more pathetic or more touching than to see that faithful friend and companion of a thousand walks over moor and fell, now so white in the muzzle and so dim in the eye, no longer able to respond to the call of the master's voice save perhaps by a sudden look up, the cocking of an ear, or the slight wag of a tail, sleeping his last days away by the warmth of the peat fire. Who can know the mental anguish and heartache that his master endures as he thinks of the day, surely coming, when he must put t'aud dog away?

The moorland working sheep-dogs were of varied degree and quality, from the purer English sheep-dog, the rough and smooth Scottish collies to the mongrel cur. All the farmers had one dog and many two. One was really ample for the majority of the farmers. It was only on the largest farms with the greatest rights of stray that two were required. I am certain the stock were far too much dogged, and that there were too many sheep-dogs in the country. Ewes heavy in lamb and heifers in calf should not be dogged under any circumstances, and specially when being driven through gates. Dogs are absolutely indispensable of course to cattle drovers, and for shepherding sheep on the misty moorlands. In the perpetual quarrellings over the rights of stray, the dogs were the active agents in harrying the sheep, and thoroughly they appreciated and enjoyed the game. There was scarcely a dog which would have been looked at at a kennel club show, but for pure intelligence many of them could not be surpassed, and would easily have outclassed the most fashionable prize-winners. The cleverest were undoubtedly those of the old English breed, and one has only to watch sheep-dog trials to realise their almost human intelligence. Some had more than a local reputation for cleverness and sagacity, and their performances were often the subject of fierce argument and discussion before farmhouse fire or in wayside inn. One I knew which belonged to a well-known local cattle dealer. He was worth half a dozen men, and no money could buy him. He knew every cross-road in the country, and was always watchfully there without any shouting or whistling. It is perfectly astonishing at what a great distance a good working sheep-dog can follow his master's voice or whistle and carry out all his behests, in such matters as rounding the sheep up, separating them from others, hurrying laggards, fighting off other dogs, taking his charge to pasture, protecting them, or bringing them back safe to fold.

On the largest farms on the most remote moorlands, one dog would be specially trained to find the sheep buried in the big snowstorms, and kept solely for that purpose. I think I knew every sheep-dog in the country, and from long experience affirm very decidedly that no sheep-dog can be trusted to make friends with one. An unfriendly, fierce and brave sheep-dog is an ugly customer to tackle, but when it came to two of them I was obliged to get my back to a stone wall and keep them off as well as I could with the stout stick

I always carried, until help came. I remember walking across the moorland with a friend, when we were attacked by two savage dogs, which I knew quite well. They saw us a long way off and flew towards us. We had to get back to back till we got up to the shelter of a stone wall, where they kept us till the farmer came to our assistance. They were as fierce as wolves and made terrific leaps in the air. It is the blow on the front legs you must try and get home if possible. The old stone-throwing dodge only infuriates them.

In the dog-fights one could nearly always put one's money on the one fighting in defence of home and flock. He seemed to fight with greater determination than the intruder, even if the latter were the more powerful.

There were occasional outbreaks of sheep-worrying, and the worst case was due to that unholy and terrible combination of a fox terrier and a sheep-dog.

How indifferent the owners of really unreliable dogs were. It was always necessary to keep a watchful eye open, specially for the dog who comes sneaking slyly behind.

A parson friend of mine was paying a parochial visit on an old Yorkshire woman. His knock at the door was followed by a fierce growling from a sheep-dog within. He was bidden to enter. Cautiously opening the door he asked if the dog would bite. "Cum in, tak no noatice of t'dog, it woant bite ye, it nobbut nips," was the reassuring reply. As he still hesitated to enter, the old woman repeated, "Ah tell ye, it doant bite, it'll nobbut nip ye." My friend, quite unable to appreciate the fine distinction between a nip and a bite, refused even to be nipped, and would only enter when the dog had been chained up.

A medical friend was once, after much preparation, on the point of plunging a knife deep into a painful carbuncle, when the patient remarked, "If I give mouth t'aud dog'll click ye for sure," and pointed to the sheep-dog under the table suspiciously watching proceedings.

And if I knew all the sheep-dogs well, I knew equally well the bulls. Bulls are no more to be trusted than sheep-dogs, and the older they grow the more dangerous they are. Footpaths were everywhere, and there were the bulls in spite of the bye-laws. It was curious how they seemed to leave the children alone. I once saw some children making a detour, and when I asked them the reason for it, they said very cheerily, "Jack Parker's bull is varra saucy."

Once I had a very narrow escape from a savage bull. He had wandered on to a footpath, part of which was a narrow pass out of a steep rocky ghyll. He thought he had got me, but I managed to climb down the very rough rocks to lower ground. His unwelcome attentions were advertised by fierce bellowings, which reverberated up and down the ghyll, and were heard by the farmers. Knowing that in the dusk of the summer evening I had passed that way, they came to the rescue armed with pitchforks, and were much relieved to find me unharmed.

To illustrate the treachery of these brutes. A farm servant employed by a noble lord in the next dale to look after a pedigree bull, which he had done for several years without any manifestation of unfriendliness on the bull's part, was one day gored to death when feeding it indoors. Its terrible bellowing proclaimed to the whole dale that a tragedy had been enacted, and everyone who heard it knew what had happened.

The following is the best bull story I ever heard, and was told me by an angling friend. A dalesman, much annoyed by trespassing mushroom pickers, decided to put an efficient bull on patrol. At the next fair he met an old friend who generally bred a bull, and to him expressed his wish to have a "reight saucy yan," and explained his reason. "Ah've just t'yan for yer, bud be varra careful, for he knocked me down yance," was the friend's warning. The bargain was struck, and the "saucy" bull delivered. Some weeks afterwards when the friends met again, the farmer said, "Ah reckon nowt o' t'bull, he's as quiet as a sheep, and them damned mushroomers pick t'mushrooms up reight under his varra nose. Thous' takken yan in." "Well," replied his friend, "it's varra strange. Ah tell ee he knocked me down yance. Noo thee tak care, he noan so quiet as a sheep Ah'll warrant ye. Thee tak care. Ah've noan takken thee in, and maybe he'll tak thee in yan o' these days." About a fortnight after this little recrimination, the friend driving past the farmer's house called to have a "crack." The maid, answering the door, told him the master was very ill in bed, but thought he might possibly see him. He went to the sick farmer's bedside and asked, "Nowt varra bad Ah hope?" "Bad eneagh," was the reply, "bud it might have bin warse, Ah might 'ave bin in t'churchyard. D——n that saucy bull o' thine. It's takken me in reight eneagh. He felled me, an' if it hadn't bin for Jack Trueman coming up in t'nick o' time wi' a pitchfork, it would have bin all ovvered."

Even more dangerous than a bull is a bad tempered and wicked cow. She indulges in no preliminary formalities, but makes one decided fierce rush, which it is almost impossible to dodge.

CHAPTER II

HYPOCRITES abounded in the land and, apparently as the result of successful bargains with the Almighty, they flourished like the holly bushes.

One type was the Sabbatarian hypocrite.

The wife of one of my patients said that her husband was invariably quarrelsome after having been at Holy Communion, but otherwise was most equable and amenable. It was a sort of mortifying of the flesh, of which the nearest and dearest get the full benefit. Another of this type was known among us as the Pious Gambler. He would play cards and gamble until midnight on Saturday, but strictly apply the closure a few seconds before the hour struck. A farmer I knew well, during a "catchy" hay time, in order to ease the thing he called his conscience, put the kitchen clock back half an hour before midnight, so enabling him to finish off a special lot. One of my patients, a retired farmer, had quarrelled both with the Church and Chapel, to each of which he had belonged in turn, and set up a religion of his own. I found him one Sunday reading the Bible very industriously. With superb self-complacency he promulgated the following thesis: "There's no need, Doctor, to go to either Church or Chapel, as long as one reads the Great Book and does what's right." "How do you know what is right?" was my query. After a long pause he pronounced, "I feel it here, that tells me," placing his hand over his stomach. Conviction apparently came with repletion, for he was an excellent trencherman, and had just had his fill.

Still another hypocrite on the moor edges, known as "Old Self," gave me a most weird and incredible account of how he found Salvation. While saying his prayers at the bedside one night he was suddenly seized by some unknown agency and violently thrown on his back on the bed. All became darkness, but he felt, while held firmly down, some violent pulling of one leg and then heard the voice of the devil shouting and claiming him for "his ain." He resisted with all his moral might. The devil was evidently in good form, for the terrific struggle went on for hours. "Self" said he became "as wet as muck," and that his shouts of appeal for help to the Almighty could be heard far across the ghyll. However, towards morning, the devil's hold on the leg began gradually to slacken, and the moment "t'house" clock struck four he let go. Shouting with his remaining strength, "Victory! Victory! Victory!" he fell asleep, and woke up a new and different man. "I war saved frae that moment. It war grand, and it's bin grand ever sin. Aye, Doctor, ye mun try and get saved yer sen if ye can nobbut mannish it."

Some of them were not above actually bargaining on the Sabbath. It was generally the local preacher looking round the farm of his host.

Seeing a likely milker the former would remark, "If it warn't Sunday, I dare offer thee twenty pund for yon milker." "If it warn't Sunday, I darn't tak twenty-five pund," was the answer, and so on, such was the Sabbatarian formula. The bargain having been made was not struck, because that would have been an insult to the Almighty on His Day—the local preacher would arrange to send for the cow the next day.

One beautiful Sabbath summer morning I was on the point of entering the old Parish Church for service, when I became aware that the vicar's warden, a big burly farmer, who used to annoy the fastidious nose of the Squire in the next pew by the strong odour of sanctity and cows which was wafted from him in midsummer, was delivering a short sermon of his own to some young men who had congregated on the grass of the churchyard. "Now come off the graves of your great-grandfathers and grandmothers and your fore-elders, and show respect to those who are dead and gone. Don't stand there, come on to the path," was what I overheard. The young men obeyed and came into church.

This excellent fellow was the tenant of the grass of the churchyard, and haytime was approaching.

The sexton of one of the churches had a stentorian voice which he used like a fog-horn, and of which he was inordinately proud. He put on full organ in singing the responses and hymns, and with such an effect that his voice was a much more prominent feature of the service than the parson's sermons, or "ditties," as they are often called on the moorland. Strangers at the services remarked and commented on such a phenomenon. "Whya deeant ye knaw, it's nobbut old Joe Jobson, t'saxton—he awlus sings for gess (grass)." The grass crop of the churchyard was part of his emolument.

A sublime hypocrite whom I used to attend as a pauper, was a retired farmer who had seen much better days. In his old age he lived in a cottage near a great lady, who with several others in her train used to visit him regularly, much impressed by his tremendous piety. They invariably left substantial gifts, which were of course most acceptable. On every occasion I visited him, and he was for ever sending for me, I found him industriously poring over the Bible. I discovered that his wife had some mysterious way of signalling to him when anyone was approaching the cottage to be prepared with this pious pose. He was nothing but a pious, kindly old humbug, and traded on his piety for all it was worth. His wife used to describe very graphically his terrible attacks of pain and convulsions, but whenever I examined the old boy his heart was as steady as a rock. I pointed out to her that this was scarcely consistent with her dreadful description. Her explanation was invariably the same, and is my excuse for telling this story. It had quite a nautical flavour. "Yer see, Doctor, he ebbs and he flows, and he's awlus flowing when ye see him. Yah sud nobbut 'ave heeard him last neet when he ebbed, his skrikes were summat awful, and his pains were despert." I could not imagine this kindly old man skriking at all. He was the only old hypocrite I ever liked, and perhaps I misjudged him. Peace to his ashes.

My annual average of births was sixty, which for a practice in a sparsely populated moorland country was a decidedly high one, and an eloquent proof of the extensive district covered. A town friend much interested in the moorlands once accompanied me to the annual Sunday School treat of a moorland church, which was attended alike by the Church and Chapel children. He saw no village, nor even any pretence at a hamlet, and yet there were about seventy children present. He was so astonished at the number of them, that he asked the parson where they had all come from. "Oh! you must ask the Doctor that question," was the amusing reply.

On the higher moorlands the illegitimate births were much below the average of a country district. When a moorland maid did get into trouble, there seemed to be a high sense of honour among the young moorland men, so that a marriage almost invariably followed. Moreover, moorland maids were not too plentiful, and housewives were consequently in demand. But as one descended to the lowlands, the number gradually increased to the normal average of the country.

Many were distinctly attributable to the frequent religious revivals, and the midnight services which sometimes formed part of them in summer-time. One of the most popular preachers was a young woman who, in addition to her gift of eloquence, had considerable personal charms. All the young men were desperately in love with her, and followed her about to the different villages in turn, some being quite a long way off, and I heard she had many offers of marriage from them.

Few male resident servants were employed on the larger farms now the days of corn-growing were passed. The average was one, and at the outside two were employed. Much out-of-door work was done by the strong farm lasses, such as milking, or feeding the calves and pigs. Quite a number of the male servants had been in the same place thirty or even forty years, and curious quaint-looking fellows they were with their long whiskers and beards, and generally antediluvian appearance. They were treated quite as members of the family, and were as much a figure in the picture of the farmhouse kitchen, as the sides of bacon or the sheep-dogs. They were naturally, too, great stay-at-homes, going to the market town perhaps only once a year, or occasionally to neighbouring feasts or fairs.

The school-mistress of one village school "happened a misfortune," which soon advertised itself, both to the whole village and to the school children. Country children are astonishingly wide awake on such matters. She had hitherto borne an irreproachable character, and was the victim of a heartless scoundrel. She was more sympathised with than condemned. The school managers came to a deadlock over the question whether she should be dismissed at once with three months' salary, or kept on till her notice expired. Half, including the vicar, were in favour of the former course, while the other half, who were her sympathisers, and also economically inclined, were in favour of the latter. The whole village took sides, with the inevitable "threeaping and differing." So obstinate were the managers that a local Solomon was called in to deliver judgment as to who were in the right. He wasted no time in bush-beating, but promptly and very wisely decided that the school was there for the good of the children, and not the school-mistress, and therefore the unfortunate woman must go at once. The vicar's wife who had been the principal stone-thrower, was cleverly rebuked by the great lady of the village for her lack of charity. Miss Frank had a heart of gold, and was, where erring sinners were concerned, full of love and charity. It is not the way of all old maids when their weaker sisters fall.

At a rather crowded afternoon tea-party at the large house, the matter came up for discussion. The vicar's wife having animadverted strongly on village immorality, Miss Frank turned to her and remarked very quietly, " At the next meeting of your Mothers' Union of which you are so proud, ask Mary Cartman how soon her George was born after the wedding, Susan Blades how soon Susie was born," and so on, naming at least half a dozen of the mothers and their first-born. It appeared that nearly half of those superior matrons had each a little past of pre-nuptial laxity.

One of my patients was a dry-waller. As his name, Peter Thirkill, indicates, he was a Scandinavian by descent. There were many on these moorlands, telling of the long past invasion of their forebears. Like all moorlanders he was thin and gaunt. Though they have excellent appetites and eat well they are poor "feeders," and belong to the lean kine variety. Peter, or

Pete as he was invariably called, was above average height, had a long golden red beard, then well streaked with grey, and with his hooky nose and bright eyes gleaming beneath his shaggy angular eyebrows, had quite a hawk-like appearance. His deepiy lined features, weather-beaten from constant exposure, were as rosy as the rosiest of summer apples.

Dry-walling on the moors is a handicraft requiring the highest skill. With a liberal or extravagant use of cement or mortar any of us might attempt to build a wall of some fashion which would stand fairly straight, but let him try his amateur hand on dry-walling. He will quickly give the game up as quite beyond his *nous*. Picking up heavy cobbles or stones only to reject them, is a laborious, back-aching task, consuming no end of time.

Pete was a prince of stone-wallers, and known far and wide as a past master at his craft. He knew every trick, and never made a mistake or took up the same stone twice. Those hawk-like eyes seemed to measure an eighth of an inch. He used to say, "Every cobble has a feeace, bud it isn't any feeal (fool) can find it." I have watched him often with absorbed and fascinated interest; he worked quickly and was quite ambidexterous.

Many of the foundations of the stone walls erected after the enclosure Acts of 1798 and 1800 were still standing firmly, but of course in time stone perishes, and the wall gives way. I was much interested in hearing about these enclosure walls because my grandfather had been a Land Commissioner under those Acts.

The Spaniards have a proverb, "Fear the man of one book." It is eminently true. Medical students who know one book through and through on any particular subject, and can quote it to the confusion of their examiners, pass their examinations much better than those clever fellows who read half a dozen books and are master of none.

But Pete was a man of two books, one was the Bible, and one was the other book. In his early manhood he was fond of reading, and in the dark winter months he spent many hours by his peat fire, poring over his precious books.

The other book was one he had picked up at a moorland sale, among a lot of rubbish and odds and ends. It was a very old bound copy of the *London Journal*, a weekly, I think, long since defunct. Through its pages ran a melo-dramatic serial in which from some weird fancy or other the author had labelled all his characters with Christian names beginning with the letter A. He read and re-read this marvellous tome of which he was inordinately proud. He could quote pages of it, and I am afraid knew it much better than his Bible. It fired the romance that is hidden away in every moorlander's rough breast. He sought out a moorland maid and offered his heart, and all that was his, including his precious books. He was happily mated. Gifts of boys and girls came quickly and regularly, necessitating longer hours at his stone-walling. His quiver was filled two or three times over.

Of course they were all named after the heroes and heroines of his great romance. Among the boys were Albert, Anthony, Alfred, and Arthur, and the girls were Alberta, Alvira, Alviretta, and Alvirina.   They all became my patients, and were an admirable and formidable moorland tribe.   And then the list of names was exhausted.   But another boy arrived.

"What name this time, Pete?" asked the moorland parson.

"Whya Betsey an I thowt o' Aï," was Pete's answer.

"Aï? Aï?" questioned the parson.   "You cannot possibly call him Aï, because it is the name of a place."

"Whya Betsey and I wanted t'shortest name in t'Bible beginning with A," replied Pete.   The parson was a quick thinker, so the suggestion shot out like an arrow.   "Call him Asa."   So he was called Asa.

And still yet another boy came.   "What name this time," asked the parson.

"John William," was the reply.   After this descent from the heights of fancy there were no more gifts.

I knew three brothers, all stone masons, who were called Shadrach, Meshech, and Abednego, and were known as Shad, Meshie, and Bedne.

Four brothers were called Leonard Peter Poulter, Peter Leonard Poulter, John William Poulter, and William John Poulter, and it was rather bewildering when I heard their names called out on the Coroner's Jury one day.   I knew them all, but till that day never realised that they were all brothers.

A very intimate friend of mine, a moorland doctor, had a faithful groom and friend called

Nehemiah Jackman. The latter declined to touch his hat to the "quality" promiscuously, to the annoyance occasionally of his master. A Yorkshireman, unlike his Southern brother, has decided views of his own as to who are the real article and quite worthy of the honour. He was an enthusiastic cricketer, and had unbounded reverence and respect for a moorland parson, who was an old Light Blue. So great was his respect that he always touched his hat to him from quite a long way off. One day the parson meeting the doctor in his dog-cart stopped to speak, and then turning to his man said, "Good-morning, Nehemiah, how is Ezra?" "He's varra weel thankee," was the answer. "What do you mean?" asked the parson in some astonishment, "You don't mean to say you have a brother called Ezra?" "Yes Ah have, an Ah nobbut had some lines frae him this morn."

"Your father and mother ought to have had the tread-mill for giving you such terrible names" was the parson's very unkind comment, as he strode away. It is scarcely necessary to say he never received another salutation from the modern prophet, as he was often called in the village.

CHAPTER III

THE MOORS AND THE MOORLANDERS : CHRONICLES

THERE was practically no poverty on those moorlands, even in the darkest days of agricultural depression. In my extensive poor-law district of 27,000 acres, I never had more than twenty-five paupers, and the remuneration worked out at more than £1 per head per annum. I treated the paupers exactly as the other patients, wrapping their medicine up, and never let them think they were in any way different from ordinary paying patients. I once used the word pauper, with intent, to a notorious "threeaper," who was very inconsiderate. "Pauper! Pauper!" she shrieked, "I hate the word pauper. T'Queen's a pauper, t'Prince o' Wales is a pauper, Gladstone's a pauper."

I used to describe it as a land of footpaths, holly bushes, and hypocrites.

There were footpaths in constant use between all the old farmhouses. In course of time many of the former had fallen into ruin, and had not been rebuilt, but with the help of the Ordnance Survey of 1840, I was able to trace all the old footpaths, and often amused a companion on my rambles by poking with a stick in a dense holly bush and finding the old upright stones of the long disused pathway. Some of the old pack-horse roads over the moors had disappeared, but many of them it was quite easy to verify.

There was scarcely one big country mansion where a public footpath did not run close to the house. It was reminiscent of those bygone days when the retainers and pensioners of the great house lived in the adjacent village. The Squire and his family knew them all and called them by their Christian names. Then mansion and village were one community and had the country to themselves. Nowadays there are fewer outdoor servants or dependents employed, and so many strangers from the towns visit the country, that the contiguity of these footpaths has become a great and real annoyance. I have often seen strangers, who ought to have known better, staring at the private doings of a country-house most impudently, and in a way no villager would dream of doing.

In one case the public footpath ran the whole length of a very large country mansion, and curious passers-by could even see what the noble lord and his lady had for breakfast. One old lord, in almost recent years, welcomed this impertinent curiosity rather than resented it. *Sed tempora mutantur.* It was considered necessary to move this footpath if it could be arranged. There was really a much nearer way between the two villages. The agent of the estate, a shrewd and able man of the world, approached the leading Radical of the district, a jealous guardian of the rights of the community, and with the wisdom of the serpent asked his advice and help. The latter, highly gratified by this appeal to his importance, even suggested a more convenient way than the former dared to have looked for, and was instrumental in its adoption.

In my very extensive district there were three large estates, a few smaller ones of varying size, and a large number of freeholds. The farms, not of course counting rights of stray, varied from 15 acres to 150 acres. There were a few of as much as 300 acres, but the general average was about 40. The owners of large estates were incomparably the best landlords. Two of these were rich independently of their landed estates. In the days of agricultural depression they behaved very handsomely, giving substantial rebates, or gifts of artificial manure or basic slag. The rents were generally very low, though of course there were inequalities. One landlord, rather worried by a few grumblers, offered to have his large estate revalued, the lowly rented farms to go up, and the big ones to come down in rent. This sporting offer silenced all the unreasonable grumblers, who had a very warm time of it at the hands of the contented majority, and nothing further was heard about it.

The dearest farms by far were those of the small freeholds, and the smallest freeholds were the dearest of all. I have known many cases where the rent per acre of the small freehold was more than double that of another farm which belonged to one of the large estates, though the two lay side by side and had the same soil and aspect.

There were examples everywhere of reclaimed moorland kept in good heart and well farmed, of moorland being brought industriously under cultivation, and of reclaimed moorland going back. These various phases were a most interesting study. It is astonishing how quickly reclaimed land reverts to type, and how rocks and large stones spring up as if by magic. On one large estate two or three generations had worked hard and very successfully on the same farm to reclaim the moorland, but not the slightest attempt had been made by the landlord to take any advantage of it.

There was one curious instance of an enclosure some seventy or eighty years old. It was close to a small open common on the high road. The land was rather boggy, actually swampy in places, but an enterprising forester had drained, fenced, and planted it with trees. There it was in possession of his descendants without any legal title. By what rare and happy chance had this obscure individual not been interfered with? If it had been a case of a powerful and influential land-owner, one might not have wondered. The owner of the large adjacent estate of course paid an exorbitant sporting rent for it.

Where the freeholders farmed their own land, many complications often arose. It was the custom of the country for the eldest son to take over the freehold on the death of the father, paying off the beneficiaries as time went on. Should he have a run of bad luck or if prices went down, he was really worse off than the others. If he died before he had paid them off, and in turn his eldest son had taken on the family freehold, under the same conditions, then the tangle became almost hopeless. Should the remorseless money-lender come on the scene, the end soon came.

A forebear of one of the local squireens in a distant dale had been a successful money-lender under these conditions, and in course of time, by foreclosing, had come into possession of quite a considerable estate.

The same trouble arises in all countries where there are many freeholds.

When farms fell vacant on the large estates, the eldest son or other sons of the late tenant, or even near relatives, were always first considered before the outsider had any look in. A yearly tenancy was much more advantageous in every way than a lease would have been and was quite as secure. Smaller farms were occasionally thrown into the larger farms, when suitable tenants were not available, or for other good reasons. I have often heard the landlord bitterly attacked for this policy, but after all he must look after himself and get his rents where he can. Some of the outgoing tenants had not been satisfactory. A joiner perhaps who does a little farming, or a farmer who does a little joinering, often comes to grief between his two industries. Again in a changeable climate like ours, a farm must be of a sufficient size to allow the farmer, if one source of profit fails, to fall back on another.

I saw examples everywhere of small allotments enthusiastically taken up after the cry of three acres and a cow, which had later become derelict and abandoned.

It was a sheep-grazing and stock-breeding country, though corn had once been freely grown on the high uplands. Some of the old granaries were still standing, and not a few of the farmhouses were quite commodious, and had ample indoor servants' accommodation. But the yield must have been very poor, to judge from what little land was still left under arable cultivation. The seasons were often so dreadfully late. I remember in one moorland parish the church harvest festival service, arranged for the usual late date, was held before a single stook of corn had been "led." I have seen a farmer bring his corn, stook by stook, up to December, into his kitchen to be dried before the fire. The steam-thrasher rarely ventured to these inaccessibilities, the horse-thrasher being still used or on the smallest farms the old hand flail. The meadows were regularly grazed till May Day, and the hay harvest occasionally gathered in September. Yet on those high hills there were plenty of instances of a marvellous hay yield, quite equal to that of the best land in England. Some of those old moorland pastures in certain districts grew the sweetest grass, and I am perfectly certain no more delicious butter was made the whole world over than at some of those moorland farms.

To-day the separator is almost universal, but in those days, which were really only yesterday, the clever farmer's wife, who knew every trick of successful dairying, produced a butter which for flavour, firmness, and quality could not be equalled.

Two of my patients used to take the first or second prizes at all the local shows, and their butter was bespoken years in advance.

There is really no comparison between the best old-fashioned butter and the best modern dairy butter. Dairies are now all over the land, and the

resulting butter is a more uniform and pure product, but very insipid by the side of the old butter.

I used to fancy—and perhaps it was not mere
fancy—that all the moorland foodstuffs, not only
the butter and the honey but the fish, flesh, and
fowl, were superior in flavour to the products of
the more highly cultivated plainlands.

I attribute this to the purity of the air and the
absence of artificial substitutes for the nutriment
which nature provides.

Those moorlands, so eminently suitable for
stock-breeding and stock-rearing, are gradually
being given over to dairying, a deplorable and
disastrous change for British agriculture. The
valuable material which ought to remain on the
land is now taken away from it and milkers are
becoming dearer.

Like all English farmers—only more so—these
moorsiders were incessant grumblers and eternal
pessimists. Nothing ever satisfied them. If the
crops were abnormally good, there was the extra
cost involved in gathering them. If the potatoes
had yielded well, there were no little ones for the
pigs. Should I point to any particularly bright
spot in the fortunes of the farm, they immediately
passed over it and told me of something terribly
depressing. I was watching a farmer examining
in detail, as they came through a gate, a large head
of stock which had been bought for him for feeding purposes by a friendly neighbour, an excellent
judge. They were a most level lot and had been
well bought, but of course he was not going to
admit this. Not he. He waited till the only
wastrel, which he had already spotted with his

"gimlet" eye, came. Then he indulged in some very forcible old Yorkshire swear words, expressing a strong doubt if he should ever see any profit, or even his own money back.

This pessimism was reflected in my medical dealings with them. "How are you to-day?" I would ask a patient. "I'se nae warse." He really meant that he was much better. "I've takken yer stuff an' it's deean me nae hurt." This was better still. My "stuff" was doing him a great deal of good. The single and only brilliant exception I can ever recall to this Slough of Despond was when we had a record crop of hay. Such a haytime had never been known. There had been no late frosts or cold nights and grass grew thick and fast. These threeaping and differing fellows actually quarrelled as to who had the best crop instead of the worst crop. After all, one cannot wonder that a farmer is a confirmed pessimist. Although we are the best farmers in the world, our climate is the most fickle: the results of much expense in labour, money, and thought may be swept away in a few hours.

The court leet of one large manor was regularly held. The lord of this manor kept a watchful eye on his manorial rights specially as regards rights of sport. He provided liberally for our entertainment and the function was most enjoyable. The steward of the manor, a well-known solicitor, directed proceedings. Twenty jurymen, residents in the different townships within the manor, were summoned by name. They elected a foreman, and usually this office fell to me. I was duly sworn in, and in turn assisted in swearing in the jurymen. The bailiff, the town-crier, and the pinder were then elected. The duties of the last-mentioned were to impound stray stock, but since the enclosure of the commons, and owing to stricter bye-laws, his services were not often required. The condition of the various pinfolds would be inquired into, and any complaints of infringements from the freeholders of the different townships within the manor, of their common-rights of stray, of turf for fuel, bracken for bedding, ling for besoms, and of stone for repairs of existing buildings or road-mending, would be considered. One year we beat the bounds of the manor, and at the time settled a dispute as to the boundary of the common-rights of two townships. The justice of our decision has been questioned and I think we were probably wrong. Even in these days, with the authoritative accuracy of the Ordnance map, mistakes of boundary can arise. Boundary stones or landmarks may fall, perish, or be removed. Repeated infringement may grow into a custom. On such an occasion the experience and help of a local Solomon, learned in the topography of the district, is invaluable. Such men are occasionally to be met with in the country, and of this rare order was the manor bailiff. His memory in this respect was prodigious, and he could detail the curious nomenclature of every field or enclosure within the manor, the many carrs, ings, garths, clooases, hags, boddums, plantins, yakkers, branfits, grassins, plaans, and so on. He knew, too, the boundaries of the various common-rights. Naturally he was often consulted when local properties changed hands, and when he died at the age of seventy, much valuable knowledge was buried with him. I should like to remark about this good man in passing. He only consulted me a week before his death, on a day when he had walked sixteen miles. I found an immense cancer of the liver, which fortunately for him had been comparatively painless, and marvelled that he had been able to continue his activities so nearly to the end. *Felix opportunitate mortis.*

When the formal proceedings of the court had concluded, the real business began of attacking the huge joints of meat provided. The foreman took the chair and the steward the vice-chair. There followed many toasts and much interesting discussion of varying manor law and custom, extending to late afternoon.

In after years the manorial rights of this particular manor have been settled permanently by special Act of Parliament, and I have not heard since of this court being held.

Right by usage and contrary to award was the origin of a law case which excited much interest not only locally but widely, on the part of owners of grouse moors. It was between a noble lord, the plaintiff, and the tenant of a freehold, the defendant, with regard to a moor, of which the noble lord was lord of the manor. The tenant insisted on pasturing the moor with his sheep, contrary to the terms of the award of 1782, which stated that by reason of the poverty of the soil it would not repay the expense of dividing into separate allotments, nor be useful as a stinted pasture, and ordered and directed that the moor should remain open and unenclosed and be held and enjoyed by the several persons interested thereon, for the sole and only purpose of getting peat, earth, turves, and stones, in the same manner as they held and enjoyed the same.

In the first instance the owner brought an action in the local County Court for an injunction restraining the defendant from pasturing the moor and claimed five shillings damages, but the judge dismissed the case as he considered he had no jurisdiction.

Subsequently two further actions were brought at the assize before well-known judges and a special jury, when evidence was given that there had been sixty years' usage as of right of a certain portion defined on a plan with frontage to the farmhouse prior to 1886.

At the second trial the judge reserved judgment, certified for a special jury, and in London directed that judgment should be entered for the plaintiff for forty shillings, and granted an injunction forthwith restraining the defendant, his servants, or agents, from depasturing sheep or entering upon any part of the moor except so much thereof as was enclosed between certain inked lines on a plan. He reserved the question of further costs until a later date with leave to apply. Finally, he adjudged neither party had costs beyond the aforesaid forty shillings.

The real defendant in this case was of course the freeholder, but in the terribly heavy law expenses he was helped by the tenants and I believe other freeholders, who regarded the manorial lord's action as an infringement of their rights. The final result was after all only in the nature of a compromise, and probably, if the defendant had desisted from pasturing his sheep during the grouse nesting, no action would have been taken in the first instance. After the second trial an offer was made somewhat on these lines by the owner, who offered to pay all expenses to date, provided the question was never reopened.

Court Leet

The following account of quaint usage and custom, prior to enclosure in 1800, in a certain manor of six townships, where the lord of the soil had right of depasturage on the moorland, as well as ownership of a large rabbit warren, may not be uninteresting.

The lord's shepherd has a pre-eminence of tending his sheep on any part of the common, and wherever he herds the lord's sheep, the several other shepherds are to give way to him, and give up their hoofing-place so long as he pleases to depasture the lord's sheep thereon. The lord holds his court the first day in the year; and to entitle those several townships to such right of estray, the shepherd of each township attends the court, and does fealty by bringing to the court a large apple pie, and a twopenny sweet-cake, except the shepherd of one township, who compounds by paying sixteen pence for ale (which is drunk as after mentioned), and a wooden spoon. Each pie is cut in two and divided by the bailiff, one-half between the steward, bailiff, and tenant of the coney warren before mentioned, and the other half into six parts, one to each of the six shepherds of the before mentioned six townships. In the pie brought by the shepherd of one township, an inner one is made filled with prunes. The cakes are divided in the same manner. The bailiff of the manor provides furmety and mustard, and delivers to each shepherd a slice of cheese and a penny roll. The furmety well mixed with mustard is put into an earthen pot and placed in a hole in the ground in a garth belonging to the bailiff's house, to which place the steward of the court, the bailiff, the tenant of the warren, and the six shepherds adjourn, with their respective wooden spoons. The bailiff provides spoons for the steward, the tenant of the warren, and himself. The steward first pays respect to the furmety by taking a large spoonful, the bailiff has the next honour, the tenant of the warren next, then each of the shepherds in turn. Then each person is served with a glass of ale (paid for by the sixteen pence brought by the shepherd of one township), and the health of the lord of the manor is drunk; then they adjourn back to the bailiff's house, and the further business of the court is proceeded with.

Within recent memory a very old man who had occasionally attended this court leet, describes in detail the proceedings. He says that each pie contains about a peck of flour, is about sixteen or eighteen inches in diameter, and as large as will go into the mouth of an ordinary oven; that the bailiff of the manor measures them with a rule, and takes the diameter, and if they are not of a sufficient capacity, he threatens to return them, and fine the township. If they are large enough, he divides them with a rule and compasses into four equal parts, of which the steward claims one, the warrener another, and the remainder is divided amongst the shepherds. In respect to the furmety, he says that the top of the dish in which it is put is placed level with the surface of the ground; that all persons present are invited to eat of it, and those who do not are not deemed loyal to the lord; that every shepherd is obliged to eat of it, and for that purpose is obliged to take a spoon in his pocket to the court, for if anyone of them neglects to carry his spoon with him, he is to lie down upon his belly, and sup the furmety with his face to the pot or dish; at which time it is usual by way of sport for some of the bystanders to dip his face into the furmety; and sometimes a shepherd by way of diversion will purposely leave his spoon at home.

CHAPTER IV

OLD YORKSHIRE WORDS

In spite of compulsory education and other destructive influences which are always at work, the old Yorkshire words are dying out much more slowly and hardly in the remoter moorland districts than the majority of people imagine. This happy state of affairs is due to the fact that the great industry of agriculture is naturally and instinctively antagonistic to all "book larning," general education, and self-culture. It is man's most primitive occupation and appeals to his earliest instincts. Any country schoolmaster will tell you how amazingly quickly his scholars, including the brightest and most intelligent, when once they have embarked on an agricultural life, hurry to forget all he has so laboriously taught them, except perhaps the vital rudiments of reading, writing, and arithmetic.

The exceptions to this rule are those who follow another call in life, or who are anxious to "better" themselves. One is inclined to think that much of the energy and time given in the school to "book-larning" might have been more advantageously and profitably spent in inculcating the rudimentary and invaluable technicalities of agriculture, forestry, and road-mending. As it is, a thousand and one useful details and essentials have to be taught personally afterwards by hand to hand instruction.

Not long ago a farm manservant of twenty-four, who aspired to become a policeman, came to me to be put through an easy educational test. I was surprised to find how even the mere writing of his name was an exertion to him. On my telling the schoolmaster about it, he replied that the would-be policeman had been by far the best scholar when he left the school.

I have been surprised too to discover that some of the more substantial farmers, who exhibited such evident signs of distress and travail in filling up ordinary government agricultural forms, or income-tax papers, had once had quite a sound, if not liberal, education. Of those whom I knew personally only two had attempted a yearly stock-taking, or kept any proper business books. What terrible grimaces the majority of my farming friends made in even signing their names. One very successful moorlander invariably took his coat off to the job. He would pant and puff, and perspiration would pour from his brow. I often heard the farmers angrily taking to task some of their offspring for indulging in "book larning," when they thought they ought to have been busy on the land. Sunday was as a rule the only day when reading was permitted.

The purest and the broadest of the old Yorkshire, which was still spoken, came from the mouths of the "gaffers and gammers," and especially of the latter, who had not wandered so far into the world as their spouses. It was they who passed on the old words for the benefit of their children and grandchildren. In reality two languages were spoken, the more modern standard English for converse with the "bettermy end," and their broad dialectical Yorkshire, which was the language of family life and friendly intercourse. Under any excitement or emotion they would quickly lapse from the modern to the old. I have heard mothers scold their children in almost an unknown language, and then explain in more modern English why they were doing so. And among the school children this use of two languages was most noticeable. Immediately school "louzed" one could distinguish the dialect in the children's play words.

"Aye, Bairn. Ah thowt lang on yer coomin'. T'lads laated yer awl ower. Ah's bad Ah can tell yer. T'pains past bahdin. Mi shackles wark, mi belly warks, mi head warks, mi back warks, an' Ah warks awl ower. Ah gotten er perishment o' caud, dhriven fra Skipton Statis er week coom Settherda neet, an' Ah's ligged i' bed sin Tuesda. Ah's ez wet ez a soomp, an' cud dhrink er well dhry, bood Ah can eeate nowt, an' Ah's that weeak an' wanklin, that yah moon mannish sharp er bottle er reight stuff ter giv' mah gud mends, else it'll seean be owered wi' me."

"Oh, Bairn. How long you have been coming. The boys looked for you everywhere. I assure you I am very ill. The pain is worse than I can bear and I ache all over. I caught a severe cold driving from Skipton Hirings last Saturday night, and have lain in bed ever since Tuesday. I am wet through with perspiration and dreadfully thirsty, but have no appetite. I am now so weak and feeble that unless you can prescribe an excellent tonic to pick me up I shall soon die."

This is an example of the "pleeans" or complaints with which I was daily greeted at the bedside of my patients.

I was called "Bairn" or "Barn" even after my grey hairs came. The term is decidedly friendly, kindly, and familiar, though slightly depreciatory, and I have frequently heard quite the oldest people use it to each other in their confidences.

Happily, I needed no interpreter. Indeed I was able to answer them back in their broadest Yorkshire, and found the accomplishment most useful—especially in securing the confidence of the children. But my "locums" and assistants found the old Yorkshire expressions terribly puzzling, and although the patients were anxious to oblige with standard English, it was not always easy or possible. When moorlanders are really ill, they are too much preoccupied to "scrape their tongue," "knick-knack" their words, and talk "larnedly." When they were misunderstood they became terribly irritable and most difficult to manage. They soon fell back into the native dialect, and this tendency was always noticeable with increasing years. One true son of the moorland, of quite humble stock, who had gone forth in early years to seek his fortune in the world of commerce, succeeded beyond his dreams. He became well known and honoured throughout the country, leader of the Conservative Party in the large Yorkshire town where he "took root," and finally a knight. I met him for the first time in his native village one Sunday morning after service in the old church, walking deep in memory down a country lane, when he stopped to inquire where the little cemetery was. He stared rather hard when I asked him in reply if he was a confirmed humorist perpetrating jokes even on the Sabbath day. Pressed for further enlightenment, I explained that in inquiring the whereabouts of the "siding ground" he was asking the man most responsible in the district for filling it, to wit, the local doctor. He laughed heartily, and from that moment began an intimate friendship which lasted until his all too early death. He was one of nature's gentlemen, serene in temper and the soul of honour. His clever, gifted daughters and son, and their children in turn, made happy and fortunate marriages with members of the oldest aristocracy. His manners and speech were those of a highly educated man, but he was full of Yorkshire grit, and it was interesting to note how, under the influence of good fellowship and when the good wine was passing, the old Yorkshire words of his moorland youth would, like the moorland boulders, work their way to the surface.

A very wise doctor I knew used to say that no doctor should employ a "locum" more capable than himself, so that on his return home he might be sure of a hearty welcome from his patients. My patients seemed always delighted to see me again, and I believe it was entirely due to my being able to talk with them in their own expressive language.

Idleness, which is rightly regarded by all industrious "foak" who are anxious to survive, as a sin rather than failing, was not unknown on the moorlands. There were a few lazy human monsters, who foregathered at the more remote inns, where they clacked (chattered) all day long, or played pitch-and-toss or dominoes, laid tribute on weary but enthusiastic tourists, or occasionally took a hand in a little poaching. Very rarely a sheep mysteriously disappeared. Sometimes this bone-laziness was looked on as an infirmity, but, like cancer, considered to be quite beyond medical cure. It was then called "Laakin fever" (with derivation from the Danish, *at lege*, to play). Anxious relatives with the appeal of despair, would ask me if nothing could really be done for the unfortunate sufferers. One hard-working farmer had a son who was a thoroughly bad lot, a typical "bowdykite," who "fair tremmled ageean" at the mention of the word work. One day he remarked that though he really believed I was a "varra clever feller," yet he was ready to bet me a sovereign that I could not cure his son of his disorder. To his surprise I struck the bet, with a forcible smack of the hand, and the unsatisfactory son was sent for. He happened to be in a very good humour at the time, seemed much amused when he heard the nature of the bet, and at once offered to undergo any treatment ordered. I explained the *modus operandi*—that two blisters would be applied to that part of his anatomy provided for sitting down, and that each night he must take one of my celebrated "early risers," a pill, which would call him out of bed at five o'clock in the morning. I also told him he would be required to come down to my surgery for a course of faradic stimulation. He took exception to the blisters but came down for the electric treatment. I placed the two rheophores under his oxters (armpits) and gave him a good ten minutes at high pressure, during which he "flackered, dithered, dothered, and shook awl ower." This very drastic treatment he stood like a man though "sweeat" rolled down his face. He took also in my presence one of my pills. It was a lightning cure. He sent a message the next morning to say that he had had more than "eneagh of that rivin devilment," and was going to work that same afternoon. Whether it was a case of sudden repentance, or the suggestion that cure was possible, or a sympathetic wish that I should win the bet I know not, but the miracle had been worked. From that day he turned over a new leaf. He became very industrious, and all his "black fat" —the native expression for superfluous blubber— disappeared. The farmer who was overjoyed at his son's reformation, sent me a fine Yorkshire ham instead of the sovereign, and my wonderful cure was much "cracked" and discussed.

In common with others of my profession, I found after experience it was always a folly to begin my professional questioning with the usual inquiry, "Noo what's t'matter?" to which, of course, they quickly and venomously replied, "Naay, Naay, that's what I've sent for thee for, for thee to tell me what's t'matter wi' me, an' not me to tell thee." It was much safer to begin, "Noo what are yer pleeans?" (Of what do you complain?) How they loved to hear long names applied to their ailments. "What's matter wi' me? give it a name," a moorlander asked. "Borborygmi stomachi," I answered. "That's grand an' comfortin'. Say it ageean, Doctor. Ah knew it war soomat despert." Its mysterious resonance evidently brought great relief. One woman boasted proudly that her mother had died of five different complaints, t'rheumatis, t'heart disease, dropsies, t'neuralgey, and the chronic."

A doctor unused to Yorkshire, if told by a patient that he was "better," would understand him to mean that he was improving, whereas what he had really meant to convey was that he was entirely recovered. Degrees of improvement or retrogression are described in such phrases as— "on the mend," "on the improve," "making good mends," or "making bad mends," "making badla on or oot," "ganning t'wrang rooad," "ganning fast," "sweealing away," "tapering off," and "pegging out." The last stage is "it's owered wid t'man, an' he'll seean be ready for t'lapping oop job."

The origin of the word "pinker,"[1] as applied to the women who performed the gruesome task of laying out the dead, I cannot trace. I only occasionally heard it used in this sense, but was assured it was the term applied to this calling.

One of my patients was an old Yorkshire widow, whom I was obliged to see once a week

---

[1] The word "pink" was used according to Skeat (1) as a verb meaning to *prick* (Fr. *piquer* nasalised, cp. *pincer*) and in particular to pierce round holes or eyes in cloth for purposes of decoration; (2) as an adjective in the sense of *half-closed* (*cp.* Old Dutch *pincken*=to shut the eyes). Whether the term "pinker" in the sense given to it in the text is to be connected with (1) or (2) it is hard to determine. In favour of the former derivation is the fact that within living memory the notice "Pinking done here" was sometimes to be seen in the windows of undertakers' shops.—[*Note by the Editor.*]

during at least ten years, for a tiresome ailment she suffered from. She lived quite alone, only went out under the shadow of darkness, and the doors were always bolted and barred, necessitating a long and vexatious delay. Hers was the truest and purest old Yorkshire I ever listened to, and was quaint and realistic beyond all powers of description. How she used to click her tongue round the old words, rasping them out with monosyllabic distinction. Of course I often inspected her tongue, which was a very unruly organ, flagellating and "illyfing" her neighbours most unmercifully. It was very broad and supple, apparently working on three swivels—lateral, vertical, and rotatory—which explained her wondrous powers of expression. She had an excellent memory and forgot nothing. At one time or other she seemed to have had a sly peep into every skeleton-cupboard in the district, and according to her, every prominent member of the community had a dark past of which she knew the details. Her vocabulary was voluminous, including many old words, which according to existing glossaries were obsolete, but which I frequently heard in out-of-the-way corners. I collected at least two hundred old words from her, most of which, as they appear in well-known glossaries, there is no advantage in detailing.

It is reported that the army in Flanders in more remote and in more recent times too swore terribly and was very "chatty." The old lady could certainly swear very forcibly in old Yorkshire, and she was very chatty in a double sense. The finest and most robust race of fleas (lopps) flourished in that cottage, not to mention other creepy-crawlies. My acquirement of ancient lore was attended by no small drawbacks, and I scarcely ever left her precincts without gaining some "adherents." She had very little furniture in her cottage, which was her own property. It appeared to be clean, because she was always busy cleaning something. That was a gross deception. But her expressive language was a revelation, and well worth the torment I endured. Seeing how much I appreciated her witty sallies she played well up and gave me of her best.

I am sorry to say she turned out a great fraud in another way; for she led me to believe she was very poor, and induced me to forgive her half her bills. My wife called regularly with $\frac{1}{4}$ lb. packets of tea, and I enlisted the help of the Squire's kindly wife on her behalf. She was a pure miser, hoarding for the sole delight of hoarding, for she had no near relative in the world. When she died, golden sovereigns were found everywhere, and twenty-seven packets of my wife's special tea.

"Baubosking" was one of her favourite words, signifying "to wander restlessly about" in contradistinction to staying at "heeam" or "yam" (home). "Sho war er reeight baubosker." "Sho's awlus bauboskin aboot." I have not been able to trace the origin of this word.

"Bowdykite" was another word she constantly used, denoting a fat lazy "good-for-nowt" fellow with a big paunch. I once overheard a moorland farmer reading the riot act to his lazy sons, or as he termed it, "straightening their jackets." Bill was "nowt bud a bowdykite." Sam was a "gormless dosselheead" ("dossel" being the pointed knob of the pike-shaped corn stacks), and Jack "war a daft dunder-heeaded feal." All jellies, blanc-manges, and "dithery steeafs," invalid delicacies, which "t'lady" or "t'quality" brought her, she classified as "blashments." This word, which has such an expressive sound, she also applied to melted snow or wet mud. "Chuntering" is delightfully expressive too, and implies grumbling or growling. "Chunter! Chunter! Chunter! awl t'day lang. She war awlus chuntering an threeapin'." "Taistrell" is a querulous and peevish being. "Naupins," a most difficult word to trace, meant pickings or profits. "Narkey" is expressive of bad temper—"T'less getherer war narkey, an' Ah war narkey teea, an' thar war a pair er narkey yans." "Gerds" were spasms or fits—"Ah had yan o' them dizzey gerds." "Nappercracker" means the head—"Ah gat er yan ower t'nappercracker an' that put t'stopper on." Nothing could be more expressive than "ditherum-dotherums" —"Ah war i' t'ditherum-dotherums awl t'daay an' varra dowly, an' cud deea nowt." A "scrat" is a mean, miserly woman, but also signifies *scabies* or itch. That native sin, in which we are all supposed to be born, requires so much vigorous treatment as we journey onwards through life, that it is no wonder the old Yorkshire has many words expressive of necessary and unavoidable correction such as, skelping, basting, towelling, hezzelling, bussacking, yanking, twilting, lacing, bensiling, bellacing, clouting, lamming, raddling, neavilling, and "straightening jackets." "Neavilling" or "nevilling" is of interest, being evidently of Danish origin.

(*Neeve*, Danish "fist.") "Clackers," "callers" (with short *a*), and "trailtengs" are Yorkshire moorland ladies given to gossip, chatter, and babble. "Slaisterers" and "hauvygauvies" are lazy stupid young moorlanders. "Ragabashes," "rackapelts," "fustilugs," and "stracklins" are all worthless, dissolute fellows. A "ramscallion" is dirty as well as dissolute. "Nesh" is an adjective suggestive of a tender and delicate constitution— "Ah gitten varra nesh an seean sweeats." "Niff-naffs" are trifling matters, of no account, and beings who go "niff-naffing about" are wasting precious moments. An "offally" chap is a worthless chap. "Owerkessen" is an adjective applicable to weather (= overcast). "It's badly owerkessen is t'weather." A "shaffletoppin" is a thoroughly unreliable being, rich in promise but poor in performance. "Saam" or "seeam" is lard— "Ah's hard put teea an' Ah's nowt fer mi breeacus bud breead an' saam." A "blatherheead" is a very silly fellow who talks rubbish or "through his neck." "Chaudyguts" is a greedy customer who is never satisfied. To "cod" is to humbug or deceive—"Ah codded 'em reeight when we war card-laakin'." (I humbugged them completely when we were card-playing.) A "cobby" woman is a well-made and well-built woman. "Desalby" is an adjective denoting orderliness. A "telly-pye-tit" is very descriptive of a tell-tale. "Tattlins," "fanglements," or "concarns" were old Mary's description of my surgical instruments and appliances, which she rightly regarded with awe and horror. "Top-dressing," originally applied to surface manure, came to mean work that was only half done—"It war nobbut er top-dressin' he gav it." "Cat-licking" equally applies to playing with work—"It war nobbut a cat-lick." "By gum yar stuff tengs" (by gum your medicine does sting) was Mary's complaint about some medicine I had sent her. "Carcase" is a great Yorkshire word for body, and in daily use. The wife of one of the "bettermy" farmers called me in to see her daughter—"Ah can mak nowt on 'er. Sho taks yer stuff bud maks badla on. Sho's a bit fleeaced, bud sho's gotten er gradeley carcase on er," implying that the body was well nourished. "Waffly" (adjective) has many meanings, viz., weak, vacillating, shaky, and silly. "Weeks" is a most interesting word signifying corners of the eye or mouth, clearly of Danish origin (= wick). Mary once drew attention to the state of her eyes— "T'weeks er mi ees air awl iver atteril." "Atteril," also of Danish origin, means pus. A "scallibrat" is a very wicked child, or a little "miracklous." "Slaverment" is pure unadulterated fawnsome hypocrisy. "Sho gav mi nowt bud slaverment." A "belderer" and a "bealer" is a preacher who bellows and bawls.

"Caigny" and "nattery" are used of peevish ill-temper—one of Mary's many failings, which her bad health made excusable. To "splauder" one's feet is to spread their progression at an angle of "a quarter to twelve o'clock." A "splauderment" is an ostentatious display of dress or food. "Skriking and skirling" are similar words indicative of screaming—"T'pains war that bad, sho skirled an' skriked awl t'neet lang." "Swanky" was in use on the moorlands long before it became fashionable slang. A "stride-whalloper" is an overgrown, hobbledehoy, longlegged lass, and a "whalloper" is a term denoting largeness of size in man or beast. "Menseful" and "immenseful" are very useful Yorkshire adjectives constantly in use, meaning orderly and disorderly. "Auntersome" is not only an old Yorkshire but also an old English word meaning adventurous. To "maddle" is to wander in delirium, or to talk foolishly—"He war tewing an' maddling awl t'neet." To be "moidered" is to be thoroughly upset in mind. "Rumbustical" signifies blatantly noisy. "Smittle" is both a Yorkshire verb and adjective meaning to infect and be infectious. " Gammerstangs " and "donnots" are low lewd women.

"Rag-back day" is the day after Martinmas Day, when the farmhouse lads and lasses who have found new places pack up their belongings. "Fest" or "fast pennies," "God's pennies" or "arles" were the crowns or half-crowns paid by masters or mistresses to the lads or lasses they had engaged at the Hirings or "Statis," and was legally binding, unless returned before day of service. "Crowdy" was oatmeal porridge, and "blencorn" a mixture of wheat and rye flour. The old farmers told me rye flour was frequently so mixed with wheaten flour in the Napoleonic days, producing a bread which though very dark-coloured was exceedingly sweet in flavour, and would keep quite moist and eatable for at least ten days. In those times occurred occasionally cases of gangrene, produced from the ergot fungus which attacked the rye. "Havver" cake is oat cake (Danish hafr = oats). "Boggle" and "boggart" are old Yorkshire terms for hobgoblins. "Meg" is old Yorkshire for halfpenny, and I frequently heard the word in use—"Sho war meean an' nobbut gav yan (one) a meg." "Souse" was used on the South Yorkshire moorlands, and is old Yorkshire for brawn. "Parkin" is ginger bread, made specially for the 5th of November. On the South Yorkshire moorlands it is also called "T'harth Cake."

An ironmonger in a local town told me that one evening a typical high-sider, living back-o'-beyont, asked for what he called a "posnet" on behalf of a neighbour. After much questioning he came to the conclusion that a saucepan was in demand. In correspondence later with a wholesale firm, he was informed that "posnet" was a term applied in the remote districts to both basins and saucepans. (Old French, *pocenet*, a small basin.)

Of the local names of birds, beasts, and plants a long and etymologically most interesting list could be made, but my readers will be crying "*Iam satis*," and I have no wish to inflict a complete glossary upon them. If I have given them enough "Yorkshire" to make what follows intelligible, my purpose in this chapter has been served.

CHAPTER V

ANYBODY who has any intimate knowledge of the remote moorlands of North Yorkshire, Lancashire, and Westmoreland, must have heard the story of the missing Scots " Badger " (pedlar). There are several variations of the same story, which very briefly is as follows. One of the many Scotch pedlars, who perambulated the Northern Counties some one hundred and fifty years ago, a man well known for the regularity and constancy of his rounds and the general excellence of his merchandise, failed to arrive home. As he was long overdue, inquiries were at last made and his movements traced to his last house of call, a farm occupied by a free-holder, who had previous to the pedlar's disappear-ance been " desperately put teea it ter carry on, an' war in varra low watter," but had afterwards waxed prosperous, " makin' girt sploaderment " (ostentation). Though the crime could not be brought home to him, the very strong presumption was that he had murdered the Scotsman, and possessed himself of the considerable sum of money the latter would then have had on his person. So far so good, but the amazing part of the story is that there is hardly a remote farmhouse in the above-mentioned districts which does not lay claim to the distinction of being the scene of the Badger's disappearance and putative murder, and the only conclusion one can come to is an absurd one. Either some dozens of unhappy but rich Scotch pedlars were in those days cruelly done to death by the bloodthirsty Northern farmers, or the same man was murdered over and over again in different localities.

When I first heard this extraordinary story, the claim of my district to be the setting of the tragedy seemed irrefutable. One perfect summer's morning, when every detail of the wide-rolling valley before us, dotted with grey stone homesteads, was unusually clear, I sat on an "owergaat" with a very alert old man of eighty-eight, who very graphically pointed out to me the various farms at which the ill-fated Scot had called in the course of his last progress. He traced him at last along the ascending "waygate" (footpath) to the "owergaat" on which we sat, and then turning round pointed to the farm on the crest of the hill beyond, remarking impressively, "He went in thar, an' it war Spring-wire Jack's grandfaither wha knocked 'im ower t'heead." He added further details similar to those I have heard elsewhere, that the murderer and his son after him would "mak throng deed" on the anniversary of the pedlar's murder, and act "the Play of the lost Pedlar," someone actually masquerading in the pedlar's old garb, and with the original pack on his back. I thanked my ancient friend for his trouble and went on to interview Jack Malthaus or Springwire Jack, as he was invariably called. Had I known as much of this man as I did later, I should have had no delicate hesitation in asking for further details. The Pennine hills of Yorkshire abound with strange characters and human oddities, but this man was incomparably the most weird I ever came across. As soon as he grasped the purport of my visit, he shouted out, "Whya yer meean 'im ez mi grandfaither murdered?" I soon discovered that he was immensely proud of his ancestor's exploit. He entered into fuller particulars, and even took the trouble to take me to an enclosed moorland allotment on his farm called Scotsman's allotment, where he said the Scotsman was buried. "He murdered 'im reeight eneeagh, an' got awl 'is brass, an' a rare gud job teea. He war at t'far end an' abart bruzzen, an' he sihded 'im thar."

On my return home I at once referred to an Ordnance map of the district of 1840, and thereon was marked "Scotsman's allotment." This was apparently conclusive. But in my many excursions farther afield I heard almost identical stories, and found also on the map many other "Scotsman's allotments." So there I must leave this mysterious legend.

It is quite beyond my modest capabilities to do even the faintest justice to the "miraklous" personality of Springwire Jack. His mother, I was frequently told, suckled him till he was seven. It is probably true, too, that when he was being christened in the old Parish Church at the age of two years, he opened his eyes asking, "Is it gin, mother?" and shocking the parson dreadfully. Gin seems to have been a staple article of his diet through life. During his tender years his terrible father used to wake him out of his childish slumbers, bringing him down into "t'hoos," and tormenting him, till he delighted the parental heart by swearing horribly. He was then rewarded with a "let down" of gin, pronounced to be a "reeight tyke" and worthy of the stock, and then taken back to bed. Such an upbringing ought to have ruined his constitution, but he grew instead into the strongest of men. He was "ez hard ez a brazzil, ez wick ez an eel, ez tough ez pin-wire, and ez game ez a cockroach." His teeth were like granite, and his voice was the voice of a human corncrake, with the metallic resonances of a gramophone. I could pick it out immédiately in a crowded market, and have easily heard it two miles away across the valley, when he yelled to his sheep-dog. He had a bottomless barrel of swear words when he "ramed an' rahved." It was impossible, too, to "switch him" (make him drunk), and he could ride hell-for-leather anything on four legs "from a pig to a jackass." He either never slept or turned night into day, because I was constantly meeting him at all unearthly hours, in most out-of-the-way places. In his mysterious horse-dealings he was like the Elusive Pimpernel. I once met him on a distant dale railway miles away from home late at night, and when he told me that he had just come from Hull, I could not have been more astonished than if he had mentioned the other well-known place beginning with the same letter. With his raven black hair one could not guess his age within thirty years, and I know that during the Boer War he patriotically volunteered for a cavalry regiment, completely humbugging a recruiting office as to his age, and was accepted, till his huge imposture was discovered.

The barbarian and primitive instincts of those of the moorlanders who had "bred back" were frequently in evidence. Some of their actions were more than cruel. The dutiful son of one who was eternally "threeaping" with and "pashing at" his wife carried out to the letter his father's behest to cut her "d——d heead off," decapitated his mother with an axe and on his father's return from market presented him with the head on a charger. The last woman hanged at York was a moorlander. It was the old story of a woman scorned and transformed into a hell-cat. She was thrilled with love for the farmer for whom she kept house, but unfortunately he was not responsive, much preferring, to her deep affection, the excellent fatty "gaufer" cakes which she made. The stupid man might have endured the former, while revelling in the latter. Having tried in vain all her arts and artfulness, including no doubt spasmodic hysterics, she popped the question only to be refused. The next day during the farmer's absence at market she bought some "puzzon" (poison) which she mixed with the cakes he so dearly loved. The tipsy old doctor was quite unsuspicious and would have given a certificate of death, had not the significant coincidence of all the farmyard poultry dying after picking up some of the dead man's vomit, been brought to his notice.

In affairs of the heart a convenient attack of "stericks" is occasionally very useful in bringing matters to a crisis. A moorland patient of mine, a widower, advertised for a housekeeper with a view to matrimony, and was so overwhelmed with replies that he invoked the parson's aid and mine to help in his decision. The successful applicant turned out to be such a "gradely and bettermy" person, that, after having well proved her capacity as a housekeeper, he became dreadfully bashful and afraid of putting the more important question. His tiresome dallying urged her to prompt action. One evening I was hastily summoned to the house to find her apparently unconscious, and while the distressed farmer was assisting me in placing her in a more comfortable position, she suddenly awoke to consciousness, and putting her arms round the farmer's neck, exclaimed, "Aa, Jammie, Ah deea luve ye." That "sattled t'job up" and they were happily married.

I heard a story of a gamekeeper who, having lost his leg in an accident, gave instruction for its safe deposit in an oak box pending his recovery, when, dreading a serious handicap on the Day of Resurrection, he approached five country parsons imploring them in turn to read the burial service over it. They all refused this very reasonable request. So he treasured the discarded member till he departed this life when it was "sihded" with him. I asked the Squire whose father had employed this man, if the story was true. "Perfectly true," he replied, "but it was a great waste of time, because if ever a lying, thieving, rascally poaching devil went to h——l, he did."

The following incident I cannot omit, though it is not easy to relate. I was once consulted by a woman, quite a stranger to me. She told me she was unmarried and lived with her mother, a widow, and her brother, a bachelor, at a sheep farm in a village which was nearly at the end of the world, and quite back-o'-beyond. It was really outside my district, and I rarely went so far afield. I put her age at thirty-five, and thought her simple-minded. She complained of indigestion, and, though her symptoms were decidedly suspicious, I said nothing, but on the "wait and see" principle, gave her a bottle of "stuff." After she had gone she came back, evidently as an afterthought, to the house unannounced. Opening my consulting-room door very gently, she put her head in, remarking, "Am I going to have a little baby?" "Good gracious me, do come in and tell me why you ask such a question," was my reply. "My brother says so and is very angry about it, and I want to know," she explained. I pointed out that gifts of babies only came through one agency. She point-blank denied all possibility of this, but persisted in her request; so I arranged for an appointment for her to come with a friend to settle the momentous question. She never kept it.

It is amazing how women in trouble will deny this possibility. I recall in passing a case when I said very explicitly to a woman, "It is either a baby or a tumour, and from your own knowledge you know of course which it is." "If it is a tumour," she asked, "what does it mean?" "An operation at an infirmary," I replied. Will it be believed that this woman, whom I thought to be unusually intelligent, took to her bed, and gave it out that she was going to the infirmary for an operation. The whole country-side sympathised, the parson of the parish was solicitous in his inquiries, offering a recommendation for the hospital, and the Squire's wife, who was terribly down on any immorality, offered all kinds of help. A relative of this woman's, a shrewd old sheep-farmer, asked me shortly afterwards what kind of a tumour his sister-in-law had. I replied that it was "a wick tumour." "There's all soarts o' tumours nowadays, bud I never heeard of a wick un afore," was his comment, as I left him thoughtfully scratching his old puzzled head. "Wick" in Yorkshire means lively, and for once at any rate this tyke who was ordinarily "wick eneagh" was "as daft as a broom shaft!"

To go back to my original story of the simple-minded woman. About two months after this amusing consultation, when fishing one of our numerous delightfully picturesque ghylls, in which trout of an unusually light brown colour abounded, I came across one of those ancient curios, a farm servant who had been in the same place forty years. He was a weird-looking customer, with long black Piccadilly weepers, and would have made an excellent scarecrow. Like all of his class he was very talkative, and soon told me all about himself, and that he came from this distant village where Creation first commenced. He was evidently ignorant of my identity, so I asked him if he knew anything of my patient. She was in trouble and not for the first time, and the talk of the village, he replied, adding that she had been to the clever Muxley doctor, who said it was "nowt but windy spasms."

I heard nothing further about her till nearly a

year after, when an Inspector of County Police
with the poor-law guardian of the village, called
on me, and asked me what I thought of her condition when she consulted me. At first of course
I declined to give any information. The patient's
secrets must be the doctor's secrets. Then they
informed me that there was overwhelming, but not
incriminating, evidence that this woman must have
had at least seven or eight babies, which she had
managed somehow to put out of the way. There
is no need to detail the evidence, but it was very
convincing. The garden and any likely place
round the farm had been thoroughly searched for
any possible remains. The wide, open moor near
the farm was a convenient place for their disposal,
and that had been carefully examined too. No
doctor had ever attended her, and the old mother
evidently had been an abetter and an accessory.
I could give them no reliable information of course.
Six months later I received a letter from the vicar
of this very extensive parish, which was a strong
appeal *ad misericordiam* on the woman's behalf.
He stated therein that the noble lord who owned
the farm, which these people's forebears had farmed
for nearly two hundred years, was so terribly upset
by the state of affairs which had been disclosed,
that he had given them notice to quit. Nothing
would stay his hand except a certificate from me
to the effect that she was a virgin. He added that
he believed the woman was quite an innocent
victim of cruel suspicion, and was quite anxious
to have an examination. I went to the distant
farm and wasted two precious hours. The woman
obstinately refused to be examined, though she and

the old woman went down on their knees to me begging piteously for the "sustificate." Two years afterwards when driving through that village, I said to my man, "Where is Steean Beck Farm?" He stopped the horse and we gazed in bewilderment. The farmhouse and buildings had been wiped off the face of the earth, and the land evidently joined to an adjacent farm.

The following paddynoddy (account) of "strange deed" on the remoter moorland in the twentieth century is perhaps scarcely credible. Moorland people, though they are eternally and viciously curious about the "concarns" of their neighbours, are slow to attempt any interference. They have a most wholesome dread of the law and its mysterious and never-ending sequences. There are, it is true, very rare occasions when the stang is still ridden to shame some prominent local individual or manifest hypocrite, who has shamefully used a woman in either single or married life. The influence of the country bully, quick to follow a threat by a blow, must not be underrated. And as far as the outer and greater world is concerned the clannish feeling is still very strong. I was called once to a lonely and distant farm to see a fugitive from justice, who had been successfully hidden for a long time by his daughter, and was amazed that his concealment had not been given away. He was wanted in a notorious poaching case.

Apropos of "awe ov t'law," a local Squire one night, during a dinner-party, received a most urgent message that the wife of one of his oldest tenants wished to see him at once on a matter which would admit of no delay. Like all her sisters she was an "aramastorky" (a most powerfully built woman), and he found her in the housekeeper's room looking terribly fierce, and nursing a huge hammer. She explained that an assignation for that night between one of her married daughters and the latter's husband, a thorough rakapelt (rascal) and incorrigible horse-stealer, whom the Squire had been instrumental in sending to jail, had just come to her ears. "Yon shak-rag good-fer-nowt Peter 'as cum owt o' t'hoile (hole or jail) an' is cumin ter late (meet) our Mary Anne at nine by t'clock ter neet at t'owd barn, bud mind yah, Ah sall be thaar teea back o' t'door, an' just fell 'im like this." Raising the murderous-looking hammer she illustrated the proposed *coup de grâce.* "Bud mind ye, Squoire, John (her husband) an' me sall be awl t'same obliged to yer if ye will be sae good ez to stand between us an' t'law." He had much difficulty in persuading the irate mother-in-law that it would be quite beyond his power to grant her modest request, to shield her after premeditated, though perhaps justifiable, homicide.

Kester (Christopher) Horner, a member of the large moorland clan of that name, was a sheep farmer, farming "muckle well to profit" the holding of his fore-elders. He had very few near relatives left, his branch having nearly passed out. No more gentle and kindly son of the moorland ever watched over flocks by day or night. In contrast to the other moorlanders he was like a graceful birk (birch) tree, growing among the knotted and gnarled oaks of the uplands. At fifty-eight he was a most "viewly" man, tall, slender, clean-shaven, with well-cut features, abundant grey hair, and deep blue eyes. A Nonconformist and a total abstainer, he bore locally an unsullied reputation for honesty and truth in all his dealings. He was perhaps a little lethargic in manner, a slow thinker and mover, and decidedly a dreamer. He was a bachelor living with his two unmarried sisters who, with an elderly farm man-servant of long-trusted service, were the other occupants of the farmstead. That he had never seen his way to matrimony was ever the deepest regret to him, becoming as years passed almost a grievance. Owing to a severe accident his father had been till death a chronic invalid, and the responsibility of the farm and home had fallen from quite early years on his shoulders. There was such a strong strain too of insanity in his branch of the family, that he rightly considered it as a bend sinister. Sarah, the eldest of the sisters, was "kitling-brained" (weak-minded) and almost an imbecile, while Mally (Martha) the younger, though a clever and "moiling" (industrious) housekeeper, was so terribly highly-strung that any sudden shock or mental strain would easily overwhelm her. Horner's other two relatives were a young cousin of about twenty-six years of age, Caleb Horner, and a second cousin, who had married years before, Reuben Wythes, then a retired farmer, by whom I was drawn into the story. Caleb Horner, who was a cabinetmaker living in London, and a very steady, diligent, and skilful workman, generally spent a brief annual holiday at the moorland farm, where he was regarded by both Kester and his sisters as their ultimate beneficiary. Reuben Wythes I knew well. He was a zealous chetch-ganner (goer) and "wardener" of the Old Church for many years, and a more upright, conscientious mortal, "with a good heart in his belly," it was impossible to meet. In his leisure of retirement he was a frequent and welcome visitor for a few hours at the farm.

Existence passed happily enough for Horner in the constant tending of his many sheep, and was like the gentle runnel which flowed through his lands. The superior and ever-restless house-keeping of his sister Mally, who was continually "rountering and scowdering" (cleaning), was perhaps the only discord in the peaceful life of the farm. In his spare hours Horner read much, delighting in poetry and good works of fiction which appealed to his dreamy, romantic nature. Though he loved women with eye and mind, and was ever attracted by feminine grace and charm, Horner avoided rather than sought their society. His manner towards them when he rarely met them, was that of a very shy and swainish (bashful) man. It is true that he would antici-pate and sometimes seek his occasional meetings with Hester Kettlewell, the servant lass of Birk-lands Farm, as she came tripping along the "bypath" which ran through his allotments, on her visits home to a farm on the higher moorland. On her part these meetings were purely accidental; but she liked this most gentle man, whom she regarded as older than his years, almost an old man, who always treated her so kindly and was so ready and willing to answer the vague and perplexing questions she often asked him. The most impressive feature of these moorlands is the number and variety of boulders of millstone grit scattered in fantastic fashion everywhere. Some are Time's most majestic landmarks. Several were close to the bypath offering a tempting and easy resting-place, and pinnocked (perched) on them, Horner and the girl sometimes had quite long confidences together. Should they by chance be disturbed by a rare passer-by there was no trace of embarrassment visible in either.

As Hester had been in the same place for nearly five years, they were now quite old if not intimate "partiklers" (friends). Kester's attitude towards the girl was one solely of friendship and sincere interest in her welfare. The possibility of matrimony he had long and sternly ruled out. He delighted to look at a healthy and pretty moorland lassie in the full joy and glory of her youth, and to hear the music of her happy laugh. Sometimes he would bring her a story-book, a gift she gladly accepted. She was the eldest of the large family of Roger and Susan Kettlewell. Of this Roger Kettlewell little indeed can be said to his good. In addition to being a farmer, farming two farms, of which one homestead was empty, he carried on the business of a butcher in a small way and cattle dealer. At one time he had certainly moiled industriously, but from early manhood his constant failing had been drink, and he was now a confirmed "swab" (drunkard). In appearance he was a "braunging" (coarse), powerfully built, and tall man, with a coal-black beard, florid complexion, and deep-set, pig-like, and cunning eyes. He was known throughout the dale as a fearless, "obstracklous" (masterful) bad-tempered bully whom when "noppy" (tipsy) it was unwise to "threeap" (contradict), or even refuse to drink with. His poor wife by constant ill-treatment and blows, had had all the spirit knocked out of her, and was now "nowt less than a slutter-muck." Whatever little affection or love this "harden-faced" brute possessed, was reserved entirely for his first-born, Hester, who alone had any influence over him, or treated him with any degree of fearlessness.

The father lived in the daughter, in her strong, well-knit "cobby" figure, her rich colouring, her thick black hair, and slight coarseness of feature. Hers, too, was his passionate and jealous nature, with some mixture of slyness and cunning. Whatever inconvenient legacy of heredity Time had in store for her, there is no doubt that she was then a most attractive and "delightsome" maid of the moor, whose charm and beauty had wrought sad havoc in moorland hearts. That she had many admirers and worshippers is easily imagined, who were only too willing to offer her their hearts and "cotterils" (possessions). But all their advances she rudely rejected, and even seemed to enjoy the snubs she dealt out. To her father and mother alike her attitude to marriage was a puzzle. The former, much "feshed" (annoyed) by her five long years' service in one place, would constantly "crob" (scold) her. "If thou weeant wed them as Ah uphod (uphold) as favourable an' is ready ter pop doun thi throttle (throat), whya Ah would mannish ter gan in tiv er bether pleeace instead ov rivin yer-sen i'bits fer Mecca an' his blasted scrattin woman" (mean wife).

Hester's long and faithful service in one place, and her brusque if not cruel treatment of her many adorers was no unsolvable enigma. It was really a very old human story of a deep and overwhelming love, and of a passion bereft of reason. In the first hour of her life at Birklands she was irresistibly attracted by the "maister," Edward Metcalfe, or Ned Mecca. His outstanding good nature and handsome face seemed at once to "owerwin" her. He was a "goodlike" man, "lingy" (active) and well-built, favouring his Scandinavian "get" (descent), with golden-red hair and short tufted beard. Good nature and happiness radiated from him. His cheery laugh, his whistle or his song was never still. He was eternally joking and "funning." "Nowt never put him about nohow." Then, at about thirty-six years of age, he had married six years before a distant cousin who owned the farm, and there were now three children. His wife was a quiet, unimaginative, unsuspicious woman, with little pretence to good looks, whose constant purpose in life was to bring up her children well and "put by for them." Naturally industrious and thrifty, as the years passed she worked harder and harder, her temper soured appreciably, and her thrift bordered on meanness.

The farm was one of about sixty acres, and Mecca, though occasionally employing a "daytal-dick" (day labourer), did the bulk of the work, and shared with Hester the milking, the serving of calves, and the feeding of pigs. The latter was up at cocklight (daylight) and a most "laboursome" and willing helper till "murking." When after a few weeks Hester awoke to the wonder of a terrible love for this man, she made no effort nor had any desire to escape or resist it.   Now only to be near him, working and helping was her sweetness of life.   Her natural cunning and wit told her it was a secret to be jealously hidden.   In the house the mistress could find no possible fault, but always praised her, and out-of-doors her strength and willingness prompted her to do the task of a man. Little wonder her mistress thought her a treasure, and was anxious to keep her, "makin' much on her," and encouraging Mecca to take her to "t'chetch" sometimes, or to an occasional fair or distant "rant" (feast).   When Mecca returned from market or fair, Hester would give him a sly smile of welcome, and by her witchcraft contrived to have ready the "meats" he loved best.   From the first he had "takken" to the buxom lassie who worked so cheerily and hard, and who enjoyed the many jokes he cracked for her benefit.   Her witty efforts, too, to cap them delighted his heart. Thrown constantly together an intimate familiarity naturally came to pass between them.

Time was on Hester's side, as was also, too, the scolding but unsuspicious wife.   The sparks from the fire of a deep and jealous passion kindled at last a responsive conflagration, and the inevitable happened.   It was more probably the case of a man seduced than of a woman seduced.   Such seductions occur more often than we wot.

It was a long, stormy, and unhappy conference, when in the absence of Mary Mecca at a "tea-drinkin'," Hester told Mecca the result of her secret visit to the doctor.   To her surprise "he ra'med and rahved" like a madman, accusing her of having tempted him to sin. Apart from her strong instinct of motherhood, Hester's feelings, when she heard the doctor's verdict, were those of a great and exultant joy that the father of her unborn child was the man she so passionately loved. She innocently believed that Mecca would be equally "gladsome," and had a wild hope that in the love he professed for her he would forsake his home. Quickly calming down he "pleeaned" that his home life would be ruined, and his wife to whom he was much "behodden" would never forget and "leeak ower t'job." He loved, too, his children. He implored her to go quietly and un-suspiciously away, promising her "awl t'brass he could lay hands on." In the stress and weariness of mind which followed, Hester's most fearful dread was that her father, who was then drinking heavily and recklessly, might "ferret t'matter out" and make terrible "to do." In darker moments came thoughts even of suicide in the river of the dale. Though she sought in vain for "heart ease" she moiled harder than ever. All her merriment went, and her "bad leeak" became evident. Her mood at first was to avoid her old friend Kester Horner, passing him hurriedly on the bypath of the pasture with some short excuse of being "varra thrang." But her intense longing to talk to him was not to be resisted. There was no attempt to confide or ask his help or advice, but his "up-looking" (upright) presence and sympathetic nature seemed to give her in her weariness some measure of comfort and strength. He was quick to see she was "sadla put about" by some deep trouble, and had a vague suspicion of its nature. All her pert, irresponsible chatter had gone, and she sat sad-eyed and silent. On one occasion when she had completely broken down, sobbing hysterically, fate unkindly arranged that Kettlewell should pass that way homewards with a neighbouring farmer. So engrossed was Kester in his helpless effort to calm the girl that he failed to notice their coming. He had just taken her hand, breaking into the homely and delightful old Yorkshire, "Cum, honey sweet, deeant tak on seea. Nobbut tell me what's wrang an' Ah'll help thee, bairn," when he heard Kettlewell shouting, "Hester, lass, what's ter deea?" For the moment taken aback and evidently embarrassed, Horner managed at last to reply, "T'lass is sair putten about about summat. She weeant tell me, but maybe sho'll tell ye." Hester vouchsafed no explanation, but followed her father and the farmer homewards.

By the rarest of chances Kettlewell happened that day to be in a comparatively sensible frame of mind. For some time he had been "hard set teea" to carry on. Pressed by his creditors, and behind with his rent, he was "at t'far end," and practically "bruzzen" (bankrupt). A bombshell in the form of a notice to quit, received by post from his landlord had quite sobered him. He had more than his share of native gumption (shrewdness), which in a man of his character would be perhaps better described as a downright and unscrupulous cunning. Pondering over what he had just witnessed, he remembered his wife had told him that there was "summat wrang wi' Hester who had not been hersen for some time."

It was scarcely probable he thought that there could be anything between her and Kester. He was too old and "not given" to matrimony. If by any chance there was "owt o' t'soart," she might "deea mickle war." He war "well laid for brass," and might help him out of his difficulties. After tending his stock, he entered "t'hoos" (kitchen) to find his wife "fliting" (scolding sharply) Hester, who was again sobbing and crying. "Hodd yer blethering. What's awl this ter deea?" he asked. "What's this ter deea?" repeated Susan Kettlewell, "Thou mun well axe. Nobbut use yer een, thou's noan surelie blin' (blind)." He "glimed" (stared) incredulously at Hester for some moments, and then with a harsh laugh said, "By gok, Hester lass, thou's a grand un ter get yersen intiv a mess. Thou that wadna leeak at a man. It caps owt." Then he angrily asked, "Wha's t'faither?" and receiving no answer, "It's noan yon Kester?" Hester shook her head very decidedly. "Wha is it then? Ah'll mak thee tell me." There followed a long silence, broken only by sobs, when Kettlewell drew a bow at a venture. "It's noan Ned Mecca?" There was no responsive shake of the head, but a deep crimson blush told him he had hit the mark. "By G—d, Ah'll shoot t'd——l," shouted Kettlewell, who now described the absent Mecca in his foulest language. Exhausted at last with his curses, and bidding Hester to "bide at heeam," he announced his intention of thinking "t'intrikiter job weal ower." Apparently his deep reflection had given him great satisfaction, because he was "ez chuff ez a cheese" when he explained his course of action. "Ah sall faither t'bairn on yon Kester. He's a farrantly and gradely (genteel and upright) fogrum (fogey), wi' er great consate, bud he's ez soft ez er turmit, an' Ah'll flay (frighten) 'im. He'll never stand tiv t'disgrace. He'll marry thee, an' ef nut, Ah'll mak 'im pay five hunderd pund ter keep wi mouths shutten. Shuttin (shooting) ez ower marciful fer Mecca, an' ez sure ez mi name ez Roger Kettlewell Ah'll reckon wi 'im some daay. We sud git lahtle (little) out ov 'im. Deea ez Ah bid ye, an' Ah'll noan mak a rummacks (mess) ov t'job. Ah's et last batten (end) an' about beggar-staffed."

Hester intensely relieved that Mecca would for the time escape any blame, was content to sacrifice Horner to her father's interest. Whatever remorse of conscience she must have felt when she heard the disclosure of his unprincipled purpose, she comforted herself by believing it was her duty to stand by him in his difficulties. She leaves the story now. Though she had many excellent and admirable qualities, her acquiescence is remembered to her lasting discredit.

Knowing well Kettlewell's queer and unscrupulous character, Horner had an instinctive "forefeeling" that he would plot some mischief after the scene he had witnessed. Although it was with no surprise he saw him coming on the moor the following morning, he was utterly unprepared for the man's extremely bullying and threatening demeanour. "Noo Mr Kester Horner," he began, "maybe ye have a bit ov a inklin' ov mi business, bud Ah'll insense (inform) ye reeight. Ye have gitten mi lass intiv er sair mess. Maybe ye weeant faither t'bairn. Ower muckle disgrace likely for t'Horner family quality. Bud leeak ye, ye mun either marry her, or ye mun pay me five hunderd pund ter lap t'job up." Though no coward, Horner was for a moment completely staggered by the audacity of the blackmail, and the utter black-guardism of the man. He stared at him for some minutes in mute astonishment. "Ye may weeal gloar (stare)," added Kettlewell. "Ye can't get owt ov it. Ower many foak hav seean ye billin' an' cooin' together on t'steeans (stones). Joblin's a witness ye war hoddin' Hester's hand when she war fleppering (weeping bitterly)."

"What about Hester?" Horner at length asked, "She knows you speak a shameless lie." "Hester," shouted Kettlewell, "mains (swears) t'bairn is thine. Noo tak notage Ah give ye a week ter chavvle (chew) and study t'job weeal ower, and mak yer mind up. Ye mun get axed at t'chetch, or ye mun pay." With these parting words Kettlewell strode away in great "belk" (spirits) and feeling quite "t'joss-o't-nocks" (master of the situation).

To say that Horner was "owersetten" only too mildly describes his mental upset. He was completely "baffunded" (dumbfounded) by this infamous accusation. His was a rare type of moorland character, though I have come across it in both sexes, an experience very dear to memory. Gentleness and serenity is its keynote, the reflex of a peaceful and pastoral life, and in great contrast to the love of quarrelling and even fierce pugnacity which is the usual product of hill and heather. Truth and honour were as precious to him as the breath of the moorland. He had a deep pride of family. Sympathy made music of his life.

Till then no great and critical trouble had come his way to upset the tranquillity of his days. He fully believed Hester had no part or share in the villainy, though he realised she was only clay in her father's masterful hands. He realised, too, that to marry her or pay the exorbitant blackmail would deliver him hopelessly into the merciless clutches of a scoundrel. The publicity of fighting it out was equally abhorrent.

Always by habit shy and reserved, he unfortunately took no one into his confidence nor asked any advice. The penalty and mischief of solitude is that mental worry is indescribably and grotesquely magnified. Solitude is no less productive of mental breakdown than the excitement and unrest of crowded life.

No wonder a brain, probably weak by heredity, collapsed. All sleep fled from Kester. Vainly he haunted the bypath in the hope that he might see Hester again. One evening, taking his gun on to the moor with the pretence of a shot at a rabbit, he never returned. He perished by his own hand in the shadow and sorrow of a black despair.

At the Crowner's Quest little evidence was called. His sister deposed that he had told her he was "Sadla feshed by a great trouble," but could give no clue to its nature, and Jacob Goystacker, the old farm-servant, who was obliged to pass through the maister's bedroom to reach his own, stated that the latter had never slept for five nights, but had paced restlessly up and down, and acted like a " strackling " (a demented being).

Kettlewell waited till the more acute manifestation of a deep widely-spread grief and astonishment at Horner's tragic death had passed, before diligently spreading the report that it was due to remorse at the seduction of his daughter. Ill news flies quickly in the country, much more so than good news, but such was the high character of this man that no one believed it, in spite of the fact that the rural mind almost invariably dwells on the darker side of a mystery, and is full of imaginative suspicion. A few days after the funeral Kettlewell went to the farm, and by sheer brutal bullying compelled Martha Horner to believe, or at any rate, accept his story that her brother Kester had ruined his daughter, and agreed to pay five hundred pounds in damages. His suicide, he swore, was an open confession of guilt. As evidence of good faith on his own part, he offered to manage the farm. He so terrorised the distracted and grief-stricken woman, that she went at once with him to the bank to arrange for the payment of the money. From that day she evidently lived in abject fear of him. In his management of the farm he took care to rob her systematically and thoroughly. Having settled with his landlord and creditors, he was again in high feather, ever swaggering, and drinking with his "bragabash" (following) of disreputable companions. Reuben Wythes paid frequent visits to the farm, but was powerless to influence the terrified woman. At Kettlewell's behest she applied for the tenancy of the farm, which had been held by the family over one hundred and fifty years; but apart from her evident incapability, the landlord was aware of the rascality going on, and refused her application. When at the end of nearly two years the tenancy expired, Kettlewell removed the two women and their furniture to his empty farmstead, where henceforth they were kept close prisoners under lock and key. He supplied them daily with food, and his farm-servant slept on the premises.

This farmhouse was close to a moorland by-road on the sloping upland, and completely over-looked by the one occupied by Kettlewell, who with his family kept it constantly under observa-tion. Periodically he would order Martha to "garb hersen up and gan" with him to the market-town, where under his instruction she would enter the bank alone and withdraw £50 or £100, which he took possession of on the doorsteps. These proceedings were witnessed by some of their neighbours who curiously watched them.

Nothing escapes the rural eye or ear. The moorside was therefore fully aware of the wicked "deed" going on, and there was considerable "upshake" thereat.

Any remonstrance addressed to Kettlewell about his wickedness was angrily resented by him with a threat or a blow. Everyone seemed to be afraid of this "bellocking" (powerful) bully. No concerted action was taken. The vicar of the parish, the poor-law guardian, and the local "mancatcher" (policeman) each tried to help the women, but from "fear of the law" and brute violence, nothing came of their effort. Caleb Horner, their nearest relative, who was naturally anxious to salve what was left of their money by the robber, threw up his job, and came north to Reuben Wythes to tackle the "crazzler" (difficult task). Any attempt by them, or other friends, to communicate with the women through the window was frustrated by Kettlewell or his sons, who would abusively order them away. On one or two occasions Mr Kettlewell affably permitted them an interview, of course in his presence, but Martha, too cowed to say anything, was almost mutely reticent, and nothing resulted. The experienced agent of a large local estate, who was a magistrate, gave excellent advice that they should take men with carts, force an entry into the house, and remove the women and their belongings, leaving Kettlewell to take what legal action he dared; but, unfortunately, they were too timid to follow it. A consultation with a well-known firm of lawyers showed a possible way out. One evening Wythes and Horner gave me a long and full history of the case. The lawyers offered me a good fee if I would send them a report on the mental condition of the women, with a view to a *de lunatico inquirendo* as to their capability of managing their affairs. They also similarly instructed the leading medical practitioner of the market-town. But a few days afterwards the latter declined to take on the job, having heard too much of Kettlewell's desperate character. I was informed that one certificate, if sufficiently comprehensive, would probably meet the case. Seeing that Kettlewell was reported to be drinking madly and, fearing the game of plunder was up, had threatened to shoot anyone who interfered, Wythes and I decided to wait for a local fair, which would probably be attended by the Kettlewell "cagment," before trying to get into the house by stealth.   One bitterly cold March day we drove over the high moorland to a remote farm, where we stabled the horse, and by a long devious route reached our destination, after crawling under the cover of many stone walls.   We were fortunately unobserved, but had some trouble in persuading the women to open a window for us to enter.   Both looked unkempt, much neglected, dirty, but not ill-nourished.   There was no difficulty about Sarah. She was clearly a "crackey" (weak-minded). She smiled sweetly, kept up a continual handshake, and with true Yorkshire instinct asked us if we would have "summat to eeat."   Martha was certainly not insane, but I had the greatest difficulty in persuading her to answer my questions. She was continually peering out of the window, or at the door, expecting the "black-a-vised" monster to appear, and quite evidently lived in terror of him.   On this account alone she was incapable of managing her affairs.   I had scarcely got the necessary information when we were disturbed by the appearance of Kettlewell's farm servant who, as soon as he saw us, raced at top speed to Kettlewell's farm, giving us an opportunity to escape.   Kettlewell was duly served with notice of the "inquirendo," but allowed the time-limit of possible objection to pass.   About a fortnight afterwards he got pneumonia which was his "deeathding" (death-blow).   Subsequent investigation brought to light that he had robbed these poor women of about £2000.

CHAPTER VI

YORKSHIRE WIT AND HUMOUR

HILL-DWELLERS all over the world have, as the natural consequence of a special environment, common characteristics which distinguish them from their lowland brethren. Yorkshire and Derbyshire moorlanders are no exception; they resemble each other in character and habits, and morally, as well as geographically, look down on their lowland neighbours, whom they regard as quite of an inferior race. There is, however, one marked and significant difference between them. The Yorkshire moorlander possesses a native wit and humour peculiarly his own, with a lively and keen appreciation of the same gift in others, whereas his Derbyshire brother is as heavy as lead, without a particle of wit or humour in his composition. "Strong in the arm and weak in the head," is quite an old and well-known Derbyshire saying. A joke which in Yorkshire would be sure of appreciation, is either not understood across the border, or mistaken for an insult. A former patient of mine, a witty Yorkshire farmer, who had taken a farm in the Derbyshire Peak district, complained very strongly of this mental defect of his new neighbours, and told me he was continually getting into hot water after firing off his Yorkshire witticisms. "They don't know what a joke is," was his lament.

I was born in Yorkshire, though only just within the border. My grandfather's property extended into Derbyshire, and I have been in practice in both counties, so that I have had ample opportunity for observation and comparison. The absence or presence of this faculty for appreciating a joke was nearly as reliable as a map. I know this is a strong indictment of the Derbyshire man. Nevertheless I believe it to be perfectly true.

Yorkshiremen generally are witty and humorous, but in this respect there is also a decided difference of degree between the moorlanders and the lowlanders. And among the moorlanders themselves, those of the Pennine Range are incomparably more witty and humorous than those of the Wolds, or of the Cleveland Hills and the moorlands of Northeast Yorkshire.

After leaving the high moorlands I practised in the adjacent lowlands, and soon discovered that the local brand of native wit was much less pungent and sparkling than that which I had been daily accustomed to. Some of those old moorlanders could scarcely open their mouths without some witty or humorous remark coming forth.

The wit is, like the man himself, of the hard-bitten variety. It is nearly always, I am afraid, provocative, wicked, and even venomous.

A Yorkshire moorsman delights in a battle of words, and loves dearly a duel of native wit *à toute outrance*. He is nimble in parry and thrust, and will chuckle for many a long day over his *coup de grâce*, when he "put t'capper on." "I capped and larnt him," is his invariable description over the friendly glass and pipe afterwards.

A Yorkshireman, with a fancy for dogs, met a friend out for a stroll with a dog, evidently a new possession. After critical examination of the latter he remarked, "It's a grand pup ye've gotten." "Aye it is," was the reply.

"What dae ye want for 't ?"

"Ten pund."

"It's a h—l of a price."

"It's a h—l of a dog," replied the Yorkshireman, and walked on.

I once asked a shrewd Yorkshire farmer his honest opinion of a neighbour of his, another farmer, who though a prominent Churchman was a decidedly dark horse. "Whya, ye see, Doctor, bottomly (at bottom) he's yan o' this soart. He'd gan to t'chetch, tak t'sacriment, then sharpen his knife on a tombstone and cut his own mother's throttle." This bit of word painting summed the man up admirably. He was a self-seeking, time-serving hypocrite of the worst type.

A stranger on holiday in a small moorland town, not feeling very well, asked the landlord of the inn where he was staying, his opinion of the local medical faculty. The extensive practice round had been unequally shared between two doctors for many years, one having all the rich cream and leaving only very blue milk for his less successful rival. The landlord, not wishing to show any bias very cleverly replied, "Thar both varra clever men, bud yan, ye can't get him to come, and t'other ye can't get him to go."

A dear old parson friend, now sleeping his last sleep in God's acre, came across a farmer named Thackeray belabouring a donkey most unmercifully. He took him to task, expressing wonder that he could treat a poor dumb animal so cruelly, concluding his rebuke thus : "Don't forget, Thackeray, that it was on a donkey that our Blessed Lord rode into Jerusalem." "Aye," replied Thackeray, "an' if 'e'd bin on a lazy b—— like this, He would never have got there yet." My friend told me this retort left him as dumb as the donkey. It was a clear knock out.

One of my pauper patients was an old lady who had quite a local reputation for her tart wit. Although she had excellent health she was very exacting and insisted on a weekly visit. I missed her one week and on my next visit she received me with a hard stony stare. After quite a long silence she at last remarked very venomously, "I see they let you out sometimes." Her landlord, the great lady of the neighbourhood, who had never married, and with whom she was a great favourite, invariably paid her a visit on her return from town. The old lady's first remark was always, "Where's yer man? I reckon nowt to yer Lundon if yer ain't got yan."

An old Yorkshire widow, a tremendous "charackter" (with an accent on the second syllable) was being pestered by the deacon of a local chapel for a donation to the circuit funds. He was notorious as a very keen and grasping man of business. He wound up his appeal thus, "Noo, Mary, the Lord luves a cheerful giver." "Aye," was Mary's retort. "But He deeant luve a greedy takker." This was a knock-out blow too.

This man, with three or four other earnest members of the flock, conceived the idea of a house-to-house visitation and mission, to bring back erring sinners to the fold. It prospered very successfully till it came to old Mary's turn. After an explanation from them of their purpose, she rose to the situation at once. She carefully locked her kitchen-door, and after putting the key in her capacious pocket, proceeded to rake up in turn some notorious sin and wickedness in the past history of each member of the mission. They had all been sinners and had become transformed into saints, on the same principle I suppose that poachers become the best gamekeepers. She had a very long memory and did not spare them. When they were "fair maddled and moidered," she finally allowed them to depart, but the mission came to an abrupt end.

A very rich financier who had bought a sporting estate in Yorkshire, and never discounted his own self-importance, had a little chat with an old Yorkshire character busy on a stone heap. "Suppose, Barker," he said, "we changed places, and that you had all my money, and I took your hammer, what would you think?" "Think! Think!" was the quick reply, "Ah sud think we sud both be a pair of daft, silly feeals, and neither of us wad shine."

I saw this man once at Christmas time, with a suspicious-looking bottle under his arm, walking homewards. "What have you got there, Barker?" I asked.

"Can't ye see, Doctor, yer not blind, surely; it's a bottle of whisky, for sure," was his reply. "I thought bread was the staff of life, not whisky," I said. "So it is, so it is," he retorted, "bud," waving the bottle in the air, "this is life itself."

An old Yorkshire squire, a retired colonel, who was always busy poking about and seeing that his many retainers worked industriously in the station of life to which they had been called, was peering over a hedge and watching one of them who was nearly as big a character as himself at work on the stone heap, when suddenly a huge stone flew past his head. "Ashby! Ashby!" he angrily shouted. "What the devil do you mean throwing big stones over the hedge like that; do you know that nearly hit me on the head?" "Oh! it's ye is it, Conneril?" replied Ashby, in great surprise, "Whya thems that's not favourable I awlus export and just chuck 'em ower t'hedge."

The very old and great lady of one village, being wheeled through one of her hay fields in a bath-chair, stopped to speak to one of the hay-makers, an oldish man who had saluted her. Not knowing him she asked, "Who are you?" "My name's Patterson," was his reply. "Where do you live?" she further asked. "In the village," he answered, "an' it's all along of ye I came to live here." "What do you mean?" said the great lady, "by all along of me?" "They said afore I came that Miss Frank was varra good to t'poor, and I've lived here three year now, and never got nowt out of ye yet," was his explanation. (In old Yorkshire the negatives never cancel one another, but serve for accentuation.)

A county Squire asked a shrewd old Yorkshire cattle dealer his opinion of a well-known farmer in the neighbourhood, who was not too popular. The dealer simply picked up a piece of stray straw on the roadside and let it fall to the ground.

The shortest reason I ever heard for a change in faith was from a Yorkshire man. The vicar of a certain parish was much gratified to see a rather prominent Nonconformist attending regularly the Church service. After the third Sunday he looked him up, and told him how pleased he was to see him, asking him if he liked the services. "Varra cumfortable, varra cumfortable, and a nice cumpany," he replied; adding, that he would like to become a Churchman, and be confirmed. The vicar naturally wanted to know the reason of his conversion, offering to help him on any matter of conscience or difficulty.

"It war a leg of mutton," said the farmer. "A leg of mutton!" gasped the vicar in astonishment, "I don't understand!" "Well, t'war like this," was the explanation. "If Simpson," naming the local butcher, "who is a big man at t'Chapel, can sell me—who is a regular chapeller—a rotten leg of mutton, then I say his religion is rotten too."

A new vicar was appointed to a very remote moorland living. He was very broad-minded, energetic, and anxious to be the Father Confessor and Consoler to all his parishioners, irrespective of creed or sect. The Nonconformists, however, of whom there were many in the parish, held obstinately aloof, and would have no co-operation. Meeting one of the most prominent of them, an old sheep farmer, at supper one night, the vicar asked him point blank why those of his persuasion did not give him a turn occasionally by coming to the parish church. "Whya," was the explanation, "it's like this. Ye see at t'Chetch, ye mak ower much of t'Ten Commandments, an' we deeant reckon mich to 'em." This was going to the rock bottom of all morality and religion with a vengeance. There were, it is true, occasional cases of sheep-stealing on those moors.

A young, conceited Yorkshire cattle dealer, whose affairs were not too satisfactory, at a sheep fair, clapped an old hard-headed and very successful member of the same calling on the back, remarking in a very patronising way, "Hoo are ye gettin' on, Broadwith?" The old man turned round and seeing who it was, fairly hissed out, "Hoo am I gettin' on? Thank ye I've gotten on, an' that's mair than ye will ever deea."

A parson friend taking up his first duty in his new cure, set off to attend a weekly prayer meeting in the village. Being quite a stranger, and the night pitch dark, he lost his way and arrived very late. He was received with stony, silent disapproval. Of all men, a clergyman should never be unpunctual, because it is so suggestive of being late for the Day of Judgment. The leader addressed him, "Thou's varra late. Thou pray first." So my friend led off with what he inwardly thought was a very well-polished and moving appeal. At its conclusion the leader then announced. "Noo I'll pray." "Oh Lord," he began, "if it please Thee give us less grammar and mair grace."

The same friend told me how he was once

confounded by a Yorkshireman's humour. In a new vicariate he soon made friends with a retired tradesman, who was a faithful Churchman, an excellent fellow, a handy man, and one who was always ready to do a good turn to anybody, or help any lame dog over a stile. This regular worshipper failing to turn up at the Sunday services, the new vicar looked him up, and was promptly shown to his bedside. After warmly shaking hands, he asked, "I hope there is nothing seriously amiss." "Nay, nay," was the reply. "I nobbut had a drop too much on Saturday neet." "A drop too much," repeated the vicar in pained surprise. Then after a short pause he added, "I am very very grieved to hear this, but come, it is a great thing to have confessed at once your transgression." "Aye, aye, I'd a reight drop too much. Saturday neet I war mending t'aud clock, and t'big weight dropped on t'big toe, mashing it up."

One of my predecessors, whom I knew well, had a very ready wit. He was a thorough Yorkshireman, and a member of a county family. He had been attending an important and very dignified Yorkshire Squarson for three weeks without any visible improvement in the latter's condition. One morning after answering the doctor's professional questions very laconically, the Squarson remarked, "Well, Doctor, I am getting slowly worse rather than better in spite of having taken very conscientiously four bottles of your precious physic. The fact is that although you country doctors are always very kind and attentive, you are naturally quite out-of-date. So I must tell you, that I have arranged to go up to town to consult Sir Russell

Reynolds, the President of the Royal College of Physicians."

"What an extraordinary coincidence," replied the doctor. "Do you know for the last three weeks I have been terribly worried about the state of my own soul, but seeing you country parsons are so very deficient in your Theology, I have decided to run up to town, too, to consult the Archbishop of Canterbury."

On another occasion he met daily in consultation a medical neighbour living some miles away. After the usual greetings, he invariably made the same cryptic remark, "I have nearly done it." "Done what?" asked the friend. "Wait and see," was the further cryptic remark. "Wait and see" was evidently invented before Mr Asquith's time. He was attending at the time a well-known and busy Yorkshire baronet, who was very irritable, peppery, and a most difficult patient. The latter was suffering, as the result of an accident, from one of those small ulcers of the skin which every doctor knows to be very painful and intractable, and for which complete rest is the only cure. After a fortnight's rest he insisted much against the doctor's wishes on attending a meeting of Railway Directors in town, and at the same time meditated a visit on the sly to the then great skin specialist, Sir Erasmus Wilson. The great man looked at the ulcer, remarked that it was indolent, and immediately cauterised it, advising the baronet to go home and rest. Unfortunately, instead of following this excellent advice, he went to the Royal Academy and then dined out, with the result that on the following day when he arrived at his Yorkshire home the last state of the leg was much worse than the first. Murder was out, and the relations between the doctor and his patient, difficult enough before, became ten times more so. One morning he arrived at the consultation evidently in high good humour, remarking, "I've done it, I've done it."

"What have you done?" his friend asked.

"I've told Sir Frederic M—— to go to h—l, and take his b—y leg with him."

One of our very wise and alert Methuselahs amused us once very much. A clerical friend of the vicar's had arrived from town on a visit to the old vicarage, and offered to preach the sermons on the following Sunday, an offer which was only too thankfully accepted. Visitors of this kind who offer to relieve by way of a sermon, are doubly welcome to the tired parson who has preached to the same people in the same place for perhaps twenty or even thirty long years.

The visitor was a thorough townsman, knowing little or nothing of the country or country ways, and there was a little self-interest behind his kindly offer. He had never preached an extempore sermon, though anxious to do so, and thought here was a golden opportunity to make the first attempt before a simple-minded and ignorant country congregation. He could not have made a more fatal mistake. There is no more critical congregation in the world than that of a large Yorkshire moorland parish. If they think the sermon is worth listening to, they follow it with rapt attention. It will be discussed by the moorland sages throughout the week up and down dale or on moorside, whenever opportunity chances. After all there is not much to talk about in the country among the men-folk beyond the state of the crops, the ruling prices at market or fair, or possibly the latest quarrel, so the parson's "ditty" comes in for its due share.

The vicar heard his visitor's explanation of his offer without comment, but smiled wisely. The subject chosen for the first sermon was Balaam and his ass. He essayed to compare the ass to the Church, as carrying the soul through life. It was a difficult enough metaphor to handle even by the most experienced, but under those circumstances was certain to land him in disaster. He was in difficulties from the beginning, and soon showed signals of nervous distress. But he struggled perseveringly on, and concluded by making a terrible mess of it. Unfortunately, he repeated two or three times that not only was the ass the Church, but it was in the church.

Naturally the sermon of a stranger received concentrated moorland criticism. Towards the end of the week the vicar met the master-minded village Nestor, who by then had "sized up the wonderful ditty to a hayseed." This was his comment, delivered with the relentless sour and cruel Yorkshire wit.

"It war a grand subject, a reight topper, bud yon bleather-heearded spoil-sarmon had tangled and tewed it till it war nowt but muckment. He said yah (one) thing that were trew eneagh, that t'ass war in t'chetch, bud he might a said a bit mair, that t'ass war then braying in t'pulpit."

One constantly heard amusing mispronunciations of words. They were inevitable on the moorland. I once asked a very bright and intelligent Yorkshire maid we had, what was the meaning of the word "threeaping." After a few moments' thought she replied, "Contradictious." She could not have given a cleverer definition and I complimented her on it. She came to grief, however, over the word *chauffeur*, when the motor cars came. She knew it was French, and required a special pronunciation. She eventually called it "chiffonier," and seemed very proud of her linguistic success. It was so delightful that we conspired to keep it going for quite two years afterwards. "Give Colonel Plantagenet's chiffonier that letter," I would instruct.

In the small moorland town an enterprising tradesman had opened refreshment-rooms, which he distinguished by the name of *café*, of which the accent at first worried the moorlanders. At one house a farmer's wife informed me that she had had an excellent meal at the cafe pronounced as it is written without an accent. "No, no," corrected her more educated daughter, "It is 'caffee'." Afterwards I heard it called, carfe, corfe, and caff.

But it was not always the patient who mispronounces a word but occasionally the doctor himself, as the following story tells. A doctor was attending a great classical scholar and in ordering an enema for the learned man's benefit, pronounced the word enēma with the second syllable long instead of short. "Oh, the quantity! the quantity!" exclaimed in agony the sick man. "About two pints," the doctor replied.

By way of chaff I said to a roadman one day, who interpreted his hours of labour very much as he liked. "I thought, Jasper, twelve o'clock was 'lowzin' tahm'?" "So it is," was the prompt reply, "and it's twelve o'clock by this," pointing to his paunch. "No, no, Jasper. Half past eleven by the sun." I saw he was very angry. He had only one eye, which always gave him a decidedly sinister expression, and it gleamed very viciously. I left him meditating revenge. A few days afterwards when crossing the open moor I heard a voice shouting, "Doctor, Doctor," and saw a man waving frantically. Thinking it was a case of serious accident, I jumped several walls, and then found it was Jasper. His eye gleamed more maliciously than ever and ought to have warned me. "Have ye got them pair of hams at Danby?" he asked. "What hams?" I replied in bewilderment. "Whya deean't ye knaw? There's a pair o' hams waiting for the first man that knaws how to mind his own business." Then he grinned diabolically, and the malicious eye rolled and rolled so that I thought it was quite loose. I threw him a shilling, which he picked up remarking, "It's lowzin' tahm onyways now." I saw him a few minutes later disappearing through the doorway of the "Moor Cock Inn."

The vicar of one parish, a former Cambridge don, walked into a parishioner's house and remarked after the usual greetings, "Featherstone, why do you never come to church?" Featherstone replied, "'Cos I'm a Methody and awlus gan to t'chapel."

"What do you go there for, they don't teach sound doctrine?"

"May be not, bud there's yah (one) thing they teach ye."

"And what's that pray?" asked the vicar.

"They teach you to tak yer hats off, when you goes into somebody else's house."

I am afraid the vicar still continued to keep his hat on when making calls.

A very distinguished 'Varsity Professor arrived on holiday at a remote but most picturesque Yorkshire dale town. His reputation and "high larning" had preceded him, and he was accordingly received with curiosity, respect, some native suspicion, and no little awe. One evening after dinner he condescended to be charmingly affable, by descending to the well-filled bar of the old inn, where he had made his headquarters, desiring to hold converse with the native Yorkshireman, and, if possible, add to the profundity of his knowledge. His entrance was of course followed by a sudden and prolonged silence, during which the dalesmen followed their usual and characteristic wont of "sizing and reckoning up" the stranger very thoroughly. The latter called for his whisky and soda, and at once launched into his pet subject, "Physical Degeneration." Having both lectured and written on this most important question, he spoke very authoritatively and assertively. Could he have successfully peered through the dense clouds of smoke the silent dalesmen sent forth, he might have noticed that one of them was listening intently, puckering his brows, contorting his rugged and weather-beaten features in a most alarming fashion, and occasionally glancing quickly round the "cumpany." At length the great man concluded his dissertation by remarking, "I think what I have told you, gentlemen, is convincingly true.” There followed a silence broken at last by the very alert dalesman. “Nay! Nay! Ah’s noan sae sure about this physital generation yer maks sae mich on.” “My good fellow,” replied the professor, “the matter is beyond any dispute or argument. Its truth has been admitted by every-one and is only too sadly true.” “Deea yer mean ter saay thet t’men’s not sae big an’ sike (such) foine fellas ez they war?” “Quite so. Take chest measurements for example.” “Ah deeant hod wi’ yer er minute, an’ thou’s talkin’ nowt bud blatherment. Whya thar’s ten men onnyways i’ this bar noo weighing a ton or mair.” The professor stared in astonishment for some minutes, his mathematical brain going through a lightning calculation, before he exclaimed, “Impossible! Impossible!” “We’ll seea impossible,” confidently replied the dalesman as he produced a pocket-book and pencil, rapidly taking down the weight of the ten biggest men in the room, of whom the first was 24 odd stone, and the second 20 odd stone. The final addition came to 2385 lb., being 145 lb. over the ton. Thus was professional wisdom put to confusion by Yorkshire “gumption.”

CHAPTER VII

A GREAT many country parsons have been numbered among my patients. I counted them up one day and found I had attended over thirty of them in their country parsonages. Some of them were my greatest friends, and in this thinly populated country, where men with any pretence to a liberal education were so few and far, I naturally sought their society.

My parson patients varied immensely in character, habit, education, and doctrine. I found the majority of the country people were rather bewildered with the differences between the Ritualists, the Anglicans, the Moderately High, the Broad, and the Low. The keenest criticism perhaps was reserved for the Ritualists and the Anglicans, and I used to stare almost in consternation when I heard some of those old peaceful Christians rave and rage against the Papists and Anglicans. Any ecclesiastical innovation which they could not grasp, or to which they objected, was fiercely denounced as the thin end of the Papal wedge. One of my kindest and most hospitable patients, the wife of a moorland farmer, once disturbed a Church-defence meeting in order to denounce the iniquity of the vicar of the parish

"

in lighting two candles on the altar table. The latter went to see her afterwards when she was ill in bed, but the moment the good lady saw him she put her head under the bed-clothes. His attempts to conciliate her were vain. The head remained obstinately concealed and never emerged till he had removed his obnoxious presence.

In the country, where the character and action of our neighbours come in for daily discussion, the parson is the most severely criticised personage; so much so that whenever a countryman is out of tune with the infinite, and feels he must let himself go, the parson is usually the whipping-block.

I am afraid I must confess that my clerical friends were very bad patients. I regarded them very critically in illness, because I have been anxious to know not only how to live properly but how to die properly. They gave me no help there. I found them very nervous and more afraid of dying than the majority of patients.

I once asked the clever and experienced matron of one of the largest of the London Nursing Homes, who made the worst patients. Without a moment's hesitation she remarked "clergymen," they were so terribly nervous and afraid of dying, and expected so much attention, while some seemed to resent the fact that they of all people should have been picked out for affliction. The next worst, she said, were the doctors who were equally nervous, because they knew every move of the game, and criticised too much the ways of the nurses, rendering them in turn nervous. The last in the order of inferiority were the nurses themselves.

How the parsons varied in character the following little story illustrates. I was attending an old farmer aged ninety, who was slowly passing away —"tapering off" his neighbours called it. I one day asked this old fellow if he would like to see the church parson. Although he was a Nonconformist he replied that he would be "varra set up to see yan, bud didn't knoaw which chetch parish t'farm war in." I don't wonder the old man was puzzled. The farm was a small isolated grazing one of about thirty odd acres entirely surrounded by moorland. Some eighty or a hundred years back a moorlander with much more enterprise than judgment had squatted there to reclaim the moorland. He could not have picked out a more desolate or "backendish" spot, and must have spent all his days delving, for rock was everywhere on the adjacent moor. By the map there were three ways to this inaccessibility. A footpath from the north, and two cart-tracks south and east. The latter, though apparently the only ones used by the people, were far too long and tedious to be considered, and I had always used the footpath, till one day I thought I would attempt with the dog-cart the south road which looked invitingly easy with its level green turf. But there were no ruts and this ought to have warned me not to proceed. I was soon in difficulties, but went perseveringly on till I landed myself in an *impasse*. I could neither go backwards nor forwards. We were obliged to unyoke, and it was only after almost superhuman exertion that we were able to get the cart back much damaged the way we had come. I then proceeded to examine on foot the track very carefully onwards. There had evidently been quite a good road at one time, because parts of it were still excellent, but moorland rocks, when once the soil above them has been much disturbed or loosened, have an irresistible trick of working their way to the surface. It was this which had made passage impossible. I found indistinct traces of the road beyond the farm northwards for a long distance, and came to the conclusion that originally it had been an old packhorse track which the squatter had tried to improve and had evidently used for a time before abandoning it.

I knew the farmhouse must be in one of three parishes whose boundaries were somewhere "contagious" there. I went to interview the parson of the parish which I thought most probable. He was a thorough townsman who, when almost worn out by years of hard work in the slums of a large Yorkshire town, had been preferred to this extensive moorland parish. He was exceedingly anxious to do his work conscientiously, but was far too feeble and frail to tackle his parish, of which the more populous half was a village two miles over the hills from the vicarage. He was besides very nervous and afraid of walking down the lanes at night, though I assured him life was much safer on the moorlands, where there were no lamp-posts, than in his former town slums. In reply to my request that he would visit the sick man, he brought out a map and showed me the course of a streamlet as one of the boundaries of his parish, which put the solitary farm just outside. He added that he would very much have liked to visit my friend, but that to interfere would be a breach of etiquette. Till then I knew that medical etiquette did sometimes imperil men's lives, but never that clerical etiquette imperilled their souls. Of course this attitude of his was a reflex of his town environment because country parsons are not usually so strict. He finally suggested I should see No. 2 parson, and accordingly to No. 2 I went.

No. 2 moorland parson asserted positively that the farm was not in his parish, took no trouble to consult a map, and began at once to talk on other topics.   There was no other alternative left now but to see moorland parson No. 3. I knew this man well and almost anticipated his action. He was very exact, showed me a map of the three parishes, pointing out that the farm was just within the boundary of No. 2 parish; was very much concerned that the man had been deserted so long, took up his staff and set off at once on the four miles' rough walk to see him ere his spirit had fled west.

It must be confessed that not many of the parsons were a success, as success is judged in other professions. Very few made any attempt to accommodate themselves to their new environment, or to create an atmosphere favourable to themselves and their work. I am told that commercial travellers are specially instructed in the art of preparing an atmosphere psychologically favourable to the sale of their wares. If the parson would only take the trouble to talk intelligently and sympathetically to the farmer about stock-breeding or turnip-sowing, to the forester about forestry, or to the gamekeeper about the owl, kestrel, or badger, half his troubles and difficulties would vanish.

It is a blundering patronage which prefers men from the town, at a time of life when they are too old to adapt themselves to an entirely new environment and make new friendships, too often indeed men already worn out, and physically incapable of attending to the spiritual needs of a wild and extensive district.

The majority of the moorland livings were dreadfully poor, not excepting that ancient parish whose glorious old church, known as the "Cathedral of the Moors," was the mother of six daughter churches. The great tithes were the property of one of our most famous colleges, and therefore were not available for ecclesiastical purposes, which we all thought was a most flagrant injustice. In my earlier days only 'Varsity graduates with private means were preferred to these poor moorland livings, but as harder times came, wealthy incumbents became harder to find.

The parson with the long purse has a great pull. "And Mammon wins where seraphs might despair." I was trying to console one poor old widow who had lost her only son and support, by remarking, "We all have sorrows," to which she replied, "Give me fat sorrow rather than lean sorrow." One of our Yorkshire canons who was a notoriously generous giver, when descending from the sick-room closed rather loudly the front door of the cottage which stood ajar. Thinking he had gone, the sick man shouted from the top of the stairs, "What's t'awd devil left?" "T'awd devil has left nowt and weeant deea," the Canon answered back.

One parson, bearing a name famous in

ecclesiastical history, was a Pluralist, vicar of two extensive parishes, rich in the possession of two beautiful old churches. He was a gifted scholar and unquestionably one of the ablest men in the diocese. His will was indomitably strong, there were no mists or clouds in his clear-thinking brain, and character was written all over him. But he was blessed or cursed, however one may regard the possession of such a dangerous gift, with a superlatively quick wit, which he used indiscriminately. No one was spared. That he ought to have received higher preferment, and would have brought light and learning to greater office, was freely acknowledged, but his caustic tongue had always stood in his way. It was feared by all, and even the two bishops under whom he had ministered regarded him with awe. The vicarial wit dismayed and too often offended the episcopal dignity and importance.

An autocratic south-country college don in the uncongenial atmosphere of a dale parish of stubborn, hard-headed, and quarrelsome Yorkshiremen, is a well-nigh hopeless incompatibility.

His attitude to the Nonconformists, of whom there were many in the parish, was uncompromisingly militant, and they hated him wholeheartedly. They even said with Yorkshire venom that he was their best friend, because he had stimulated their opposition and strengthened their forces so that they were enabled to build their formidable temple.

I invariably received the greatest kindness and courtesy from him, and had a deep respect for his transcendent ability. Only once I came up against it, and though my will prevailed, it was a moral annihilation.

It was one of those rare occasions when a doctor takes the very grave responsibility of excluding for the time being a minister of religion from the sick-room. When a patient is *in extremis* and there is no hope of recovery, the doctor is compelled by every moral and ethical law to allow the presence of a spiritual consoler. But the doctor's standpoint is, that while hope remains, he must exclude any influence which he thinks is inimical to recovery. His most dangerous enemy is fear, fear of suffering, and specially fear of death, and it unfortunately happens sometimes that the presence of the minister in the sick-room is to the patient a symbol of the King of Terrors. This is more often so in the case of the young. Some ministers, and specially Church parsons, literally exhort and pray *ex cathedrâ*, with a volume of voice that can often be heard outside the house. Some linger far too long. This particular case was one of sudden dangerous hæmorrhage in a young woman, a visitor to a house close to the vicarage, the church, and my house. She was engaged to be married and intensely anxious to get better. The most absolute rest and quiet was her only chance. One day she begged me to ask the curate to discontinue his visits, complaining not only that his voice was too penetrating, but that his coming made her fearful and afraid of death, bringing on palpitation.

I saw my great friend the curate-in-charge, and begged him to discontinue his visits, explaining my reasons for doing so; but unfortunately he took my interference very badly, and angrily protested that we doctors rated the vile body far too highly, when the safety of the soul was above all other considerations. The expected happened. Called to a second violent hæmorrhage I saw in the tail of my eye the parson just disappearing into his parsonage as I hurried to my patient. When the nurse told me the hæmorrhage had recurred during the parson's prayer, the *fiat* went forth that no one should be admitted into the sick-room without my permission. My parson friend and I had a very stormy interview afterwards, our only real great quarrel during a long friendship. In high spleen he suddenly decided to go off on a holiday and remove himself from such an atmosphere of annoyance and mortification. The patient became so critically ill that on the following Sunday the church-wardens at my request agreed to ring only the lightest of the old church bells, for a few seconds. The first question the vicar asked the church-wardens when he arrived from his distant vicarage to take the service, was why the usual peal of bells was not being rung, and, on hearing the reason, remarked that he would go and see the patient directly after service. The church-wardens smiled but explained nothing. He entered the house of sickness as was his wont, first knocking gently at the door and then proceeded unasked upstairs. But a guardian angel was there and barred the way.

"There is someone dangerously ill here," the vicar remarked.

"Yes," replied the guardian angel, "but I have strict orders not to admit anybody to the sick-room."

" Whose orders pray ? "

" Dr Bishop's."

" Oh ! Dr Bishop's. Well, if Dr Bishop cannot save the patient, it is no use God Almighty trying. Good-morning."

The patient made an excellent recovery, and is now a happy grandmother.

It was on the occasion of an afternoon Confirmation service, when on the point of sitting down with a party of guests to a well-furnished lunch table, that the same divine received a prepaid telegram from the bishop asking the hour of Confirmation. "That's the kind of bishop we have who doesn't even know his own official appointments," scornfully exclaimed the vicar as he sent the form fluttering to the floor. "I shall not answer it." Perhaps he was rather hungry and therefore rather angry. Towards the end of the feast, when the good red wine had passed round and all were feeling happy, a guest who was devoted to the bishop, asked, "Don't you think, vicar, the wire requires an answer as a mere matter of courtesy?" "Perhaps it does," was the reply, as he picked up the form and thereon wrote very quickly, "Time of Confirmation—my time three o'clock—official time not known."

The bishop really deserved the vicarial rebuke ; he was much more of a courtier than a diocesan.

I once heard the vicar get the better of an old stubborn Yorkshire farmer, who disliked him very much, and whom he had asked for his annual subscription to some parish object before the end of the financial year.

" I never pays aforehand," said the farmer.

"Are you sure?"

"Never in a week o' Sundays; nobbut feeals pay aforehand."

"Oh I suppose you never put stamps on your letters; always pay at the end of railway journeys and all entertainments." He left the farmer speechless.

The uncle of a moorlander had died in a distant workhouse, and there had been some unavoidable delay about his burial in the family grave in the old churchyard. The nephew called on the vicar to arrange about the final interment. Naturally a "threeaper," his temper was not improved by being kept waiting some time, and it was in no amiable mood that he addressed the vicar, " Noo thens, we sall bring t'aud lad ten miles by t'road, an' we reckon we sall be at t'chetch by three by t'clock or rather mair for t'sahding ter morrow arterean." The vicar, who was not a man to accept dictation, replied very decidedly, "Oh! what about my convenience in the matter? You cannot have funerals just when you think fit."

"We're noan patickler ter half an hour or mair," suggested the moorlander.

"I cannot possibly take the funeral to-morrow afternoon," was the uncompromising answer.

"Thou meeans thou weeant try an' mannish it. I tell thee what, other foalk can be ez meean ez muckment teea. I'll warrant ye we sall bring t'aud lad along in his box, an' if thou weeant hap t'job up, then we sall upend him ageean t'chetch door, and thou can sahd him whenever thou's amind." With this ultimatum the stubborn Yorkshireman strode away. The funeral took place at three o'clock the following afternoon without further ado.

To be powerful in prayer was the highest attainment of the local preacher. Great lung power, described by the wicked as beldering (bellowing) or ranting, was the first great essential. The second great essential was the use of occasional long pauses in the prayer, and of emotional pianos, crescendos, and fortissimos. Too easy or affected (knick-knacking) fluency was suggestive of the ready-prepared prayers of the Established Church, and therefore a decided disqualification. The less grammar the better. The crucial test of excellence was the extent of responsive "gerning" (groaning) from the travailing and wrestling suppliants.

One very gentle, kindly, and delightful old man, the Nestor of the local preachers, was a marked exception to this general rule of shouting, though he regarded power in prayer as the highest qualification. He and his forebears had owned and farmed the same land for at least four hundred years, and had deeds to prove it. One forebear had been the vicar of the old parish. Perhaps his long and respectable descent accounted for his gentleness of speech. He was recovering from a long illness I had been attending him for, when one day he asked, "Does Mr Linacre come to see you?" Mr Linacre was the parson, and the greatest friendship existed between us. I replied at once, "Yes! We are the greatest friends. We take long walks together over the moors and we go a-fishing together." "No! no!" he asked again, "does he come to see you?" I could not make out what the old boy was driving at, so I replied that he called nearly every morning just after breakfast for a few minutes' chat, to ask who were ill. "No! no! Does he come to see you? Does he give you spiritual consolation?" He rolled out the spiritual with unctuous satisfaction. Now my friend was a most manly, straightforward, stand-no-nonsense Christian pastor, who never hesitated to talk to me for my soul's good, or even occasionally offer me a little whisky for my bodily good. I could answer quite truthfully a decided "Yes." Then his next question was, "Do you think he is powerful in prayer?" This was rather a poser, but I answered, "Yes, quite above the average." "Well," replied the old preacher, "t'man's reet eneagh, an' a good liver, bud he puts nae power in his prayer. He gat agate ower quick an' knick-knacked it ower fine. It war high larned bud thar war no boddums in it, and Ah nobbut gerned yance when he came to see me to-day."

When I told the parson the story the same evening, he was much amused and not a little chagrined, because it appeared he had specially prepared an "extempore" prayer, and had left the sick man feeling rather proud of his effort. Probably there had been too much good grammar in it.

I found the families of the county squires incomparably the most agreeable and satisfactory patients to attend. Once their confidence gained, they were the most loyal and considerate of friends and supporters.

One great drawback in attending at the large houses was the valuable time lost in running the gauntlet of so many flunkeys. Attending a great lady, I was conducted from the front door to the library by a footman, from the library to Miladi's boudoir by the butler, from the boudoir to a dressing-room by her maid, and from the latter to the sick-room by the nurse. Time twenty minutes. The next morning I walked up unannounced to Miladi's bedroom and knocked at the door.

"Who is there?" asked Miladi.

"The doctor," I answered.

"Oh I'm not ready," she protested, but I told her I was anxious to see her when she was not ready, so that I could more easily judge of her true condition. This making of the patient ready and pretty by fastidious nurses is often very deceptive. I remember well a case where a specialist saw a patient who, after being made ready and pretty, pulled himself together in extraordinary fashion although desperately ill. To our astonishment the great man gave a most favourable prognosis, only to have the mortification after lunch of reversing it. The patient died the next day.

The gentlefolk had nothing of the silly modesty about the functions of their bodies, which is so evident among the middle classes. Many of the latter would lower their voices to a whisper and look so very mysterious that one might think some momentous secret was on the point of revelation.

They never gave each other away, however much they depreciated some of their neighbours, and they never pressed one to eat, which was a great relief in this tenaciously hospitable country. They boasted perhaps too much about the antiquity of their families. But after all this was excusable. Pride of race is instinctive and immemorial, and in these days when the old families are being rapidly taxed out of their lands, it is the only heritage that is left. Did not two Scotchmen named Grant and Macpherson once have a fierce discussion on the antiquity of their respective families? The former possessed a family Bible in which by some strange accident there was a misprint, which stated that "there were Grants (instead of giants) in those days." He proudly pointed out this irrefutable proof of the antiquity of the Grants, and at the same time the fact that there was no mention of the Macphersons in the Ark. "Hoots mun," replied Macpherson, "the Macpheersons had a bait o' their ain."

They boasted too of their wine, though not in the unblushing fashion of the profiteer. That was equally excusable. When one swallows a curio, its description makes it still more delectable. There is something, though, rather pathetic about the drinking of very old wines. While they exist, they are curios to be proud of, but when they have been consumed they have vanished for ever.

After all, the English aristocracy of the land is the most virile in the world.

Even the most bitter and irreconcilable of the country Radicals always professed to have a soft place in their political hearts for what they called the "Old Originals," the old county families, though how they could always distinguish them was not quite clear, seeing that the absorption of landed aristocracy by plutocracy has been going on steadily for centuries. They, however, discriminated in their favour, and even sometimes went so far as to suggest that if all the country aristocracy were up to the high level of the old families, the *raison d'être* of their Radicalism would no longer exist. One specially militant old Radical, who had prospered exceedingly in life, used to boast with pride how his father had made the coffin of a great territorial lady landowner. I wondered at his being so proud of it, because this particular high-crusted Tory lady, when her nominee had been rejected in her pocket borough at the Reform Election of 1832, took a very high-handed revenge by turning out all her tenants, and stopping the pension of all those who had had the hardihood to vote against her interest. That the Yorkshire moorlanders were the most stubborn of politicians it is easy to understand. One never heard of conversion. So pig-headed and obstinate were they, I used to say that if they died and rose again they would still not believe.

How men, level-headed and well-balanced enough in the ordinary affairs of life, can be so unreasonable in their outlook on politics and religion, is one of the most puzzling of enigmas.

I was struck in general with the devoted friendship and love which these old families had for their long-tried and well-trusted servants, though I often wondered how the old squires, who were professedly good Christian churchmen, reconciled their exclusiveness on this earth with the probably democratic atmosphere of the Kingdom of Heaven. I remember a widow showing me a letter she had received from a squire on the death of her husband, an old retainer. It was a touching kindly letter, referring to the man's long faithful service; but the writer went on to say that he looked forward to sitting near the deceased in Heaven, and evidently contemplated an intimacy which he would not have entertained for a moment on earth. On the other hand I remember one old squire referring to an old family nurse thus, "Though she were armless and legless and perfectly helpless, still she shall have a home of comfort and happiness with us till she dies."

A great lady of old family, the queen of her village and kingdom, Miss Frank, literally gave all she had to the sick and the poor, after the immediate requirements of her establishment had been met. That she might more readily know exactly how much she could spare for them, she insisted on paying all her accounts, including mine, every month. She was downright and thorough in all her methods, full of commonsense, with great breadth of mind, and almost sledge-hammer decision. Human love and charity were conspicuous in her, and to all erring sinners she was mercifully tolerant. But hypocrisy and religious cant were an utter abomination to her and excited her scorn. She lived to the ripe age of ninety, though in later years she was crippled by rheumatism which prevented her, to her great grief, from attending the village church, built and endowed by her father. One day there came to her the personification of sanctimonious cant, the vicar's wife's mother.

"Are you not deeply sorry, Miss Frank," said the latter, "that you cannot come to the dear church again?"

"On the contrary," snapped Miss Frank, "I

am very pleased that I have not the vicar's dry windy old sermons to listen to."

A painful pause was followed by another attempt, "What a blessed consolation it must be that you are still able to read the Blessed Book instead."

"I never read the Bible."

A still more painful pause. Then—"Oh, how overjoyed you must be that each day brings you nearer to Heaven."

"I don't wish to die," rasped Miss Frank. "I want to live as long as I can, and when I do die I am going to Hell. I shall meet possibly more of my friends there than in Heaven." Such was her uncompromising mood, as she put the vicar's wife's mother to flight.

When her maid of forty years' faithful service and companion of many journeyings abroad, whom she loved most dearly, was dying from painful cancer, she was terribly anxious that she should die quickly and escape from her torment and suffering. Each day came the impatient question, if she was nearer the end. I believe if I had poisoned her straight off she would have warmly thanked me and offered me a handsome fee. I cannot say that I was unsympathetic to this attitude of hers towards hopeless and almost helpless suffering. In fact quite the contrary. Unless the patient himself expressly wishes it, I have never acquiesced in the practice of keeping these cases alive by concentrated foods and strong drugs, and am thankful to confess have occasionally helped and speeded them on their journey. It is too often the loving and solicitous relations, who would not hesitate two moments about putting out of the way a favourite dog or horse under the same circumstances, who selfishly insist on this purposeless prolongation of life, and I hope the day will come when painless extinction of hopeless suffering will be legalised.

One old squire whom I attended was well known throughout the country, and had character written all over his face. In the early days he had been in the Navy, but afterwards settled down in the county, farming a considerable portion of his own estate. He loved all the old expressive Yorkshire words, and, with his wondrous gift of mimicry, was inimitable in telling a good Yorkshire story. His gift of language, in his case an hereditary endowment, was a revelation, and in exhorting his retainers to a due and proper appreciation of their duties, could serve him for a good ten minutes without repetition.

I once went to see him in a nursing home where he had been some weeks. "Don't you find it very dull, Squire?" I asked. "Dull! Not a bit," he replied, "I have been inventing some more Yorkshire swear-words. I am afraid all my old ones have lost their sting."

Some of the old squires I knew were quite proud of their old Yorkshire, and often talked it as broadly as possible in addressing the herd. One, a baronet, who unfortunately drank heavily, and was often carried to bed in a helpless state by one of my friends, was chairman of the bench of magistrates in his district, but for a long time had dealt out justice in a ridiculously lenient fashion, carrying matters with a very high hand.

At last his brother magistrates, tired of being ignored, held an indignation meeting, threatening to report him to the Lord Chancellor unless he mended his ways. He was very contrite, promising immediate amendment, but at the very next case which came before him, completely forgot his promise. It was a double one of assault and drunkenness. He thus pronounced sentence to the offending Yorkshire man. "Noo thens, for t'assault we'll fine yer a shilling and costs. As for t'drunkenness we'll say nowt about it, as we get drunk oorsells."

This story recalls another. An habitual drunkard, taking stock of the bench of magistrates assembled to try his case, commented rather audibly to himself. "I don't care a damn for aud Pollard," naming one of them. Unfortunately this remark was overheard by old Pollard, who retorted, "And aud Pollard doesn't care a damn for thee."

Some sixty years ago a local and most autocratic squarson, who was the proprietor of all the land, the houses, the trees, the rivulets, the church, and everything pertaining to his village except the canopy of the sky, took to task, as he hurried to take the Sunday morning service, a villager who had long annoyed him by never attending church. On the great Day of Rest many Christians are often dreadfully austere and stern, and the Squire-Parson was particularly so that morning. "You never come to church, Thwaite," he said angrily. "Telling me weeant mak onny better of t'job," replied the stubborn Yorkshire tyke. "I will make you come to church," threatened the parson. "Thou weeant deea nowt o' t'soart, an' thou weeant mak me gan to t'chetch." "I will. If you don't come to church, I will turn you out of your cottage."

"Damn ye, Ah tell yer Ah weeant gan to t'chetch an' neabody will mak me," shouted Thwaite, as he turned his back on the parson, who strode on to the House of Prayer, full of holy wrath.

He summoned the man the following week, before the local court on the charge of using profane language, and the case came before two local magistrates, a famous sporting baronet and a retired army captain. Both these magistrates, who were very hard swearers themselves, and had taken a double first in maledictory philology, were much exercised in mind when they had heard the evidence. They secretly sympathised with the offender, and in their long consultation afterwards were delighted in finding a way out. The Baronet thus delivered judgment, "Now, Thwaite, you certainly used very bad language, but not profane language. If you had said 'God damn you,' that would have been profanity, but as you only said 'Damn you,' we dismiss the case."

CHAPTER VIII

THE director of ceremonies at an important Yorkshire moorland funeral was busily engaged in instructing the numerous gathering of family and other mourners regarding the bestowal of their persons in the crowded array of conveyances provided for the occasion. "Mr Parnaby," he directed, "will drive with Mrs Umpleby in the dog-cart behind the piebald." Now it happened that Mrs Umpleby was Mr Parnaby's mother-in-law, and his features, which up to that moment had worn a rather solemn but otherwise pleasant and expectant look, became suddenly clouded over, and he remarked in lugubrious and doleful accents, "If I have to drive with she I shan't enjoy myself a bit."

This honest, if rude remark of Mr Parnaby explains very briefly how Yorkshiremen, and specially dalesmen and moorsiders, think of funerals. They "enjoy" every detail of the rite, the farewell look at the "corpse," the drive to and from the moorland church, the society of their fellow-mourners, the stories and anecdotes told of "the corpse's" worth and virtues, and above all, the big feast of Yorkshire ham and funeral baked meats at the end.

They look forward to it with pleasant feelings of expectation; they wonder who will be there from up the dale or over the moor, and they speculate as to the worldly possessions "the corpse" will leave behind him. By way of working up the interest they would exaggerate the wealth of their deceased neighbour. "Mr Richmond or Mr Verity," they would say, "will cut up for thousands"; but at the final dissection of these gentlemen it was more usually a case of hundreds.

They would rather miss a favourite fair or a tempting sale than an important family burying, and were much disappointed when rain or snow-storm marred their pleasure.

Although it is quite usual among lowlanders and lowsiders to exaggerate their woe on these occasions, I saw few manifestations of the sort among their hardier high-side brothers. More than once I have closely scanned every face in a packed moorland church and not seen the slightest sign of emotion. If anything, their demeanour was sterner and harder than usual. It was tearless grief. Only here and there a hot scalding tear would force its way out despite all contortion of rugged features.

When the departed had died rich in years, he was worn out and done, and it was all in the course of nature; over one younger in years genuine regret would be expressed that he had slipped away so early. "It war a pity," was the laconic formula.

When on these occasions the feast of the body is at length ended, there follows the feast of the mind and flow of reason mid blinding clouds of tobacco smoke. Provided the testamentary bequests of the "corpse" are just, fair, and satisfactory to all concerned, the utmost harmony and good fellowship prevail.

Stories innumerable, long- and short-winded, are recounted of his skill in bargaining, his sound judgment of a horse, his wondrous sheep dogs, the days of his courtship, the birth of his first-born, incidents of great snowstorms, of long lost and buried sheep, of good and bad hay harvests, and of all the important events of his life. Then one by one these friends from early youth will yoke up and drive quietly away. Some of them, perhaps, have come thirty or forty miles from a far-off dale, and the weather may be dark and stormy.

One of my patients was buried in a distant dale, and on the return journey the mourners were overtaken by a terrible blizzard. Some of the more delicately constituted had to take refuge in the hearse, in which, closely packed together, they eventually arrived home in safety.

Should, however, the last will and testament of the "corpse" be manifestly unjust, vindictive, or a blow to schemers, then it is quite another story. There is an atmosphere of lowering clouds. The interested mourners maintain their wonted taciturnity and stern demeanour; the ham is consumed in grim silence, broken now and again perhaps with acrimonious and angry remarks, hissed out with much snarling and pouting. There is a declaration of war, secret or open, and the quarrel commenced that day between the various members of the family and their sympathising connections and friends, will be maintained bitterly and relentlessly till death.

It is impossible for a country doctor to refuse the sudden demands that are occasionally sprung upon him to make the will of a dying patient. The schoolmaster, the parson or other educated person may not be immediately available and the patient is obviously *in extremis*. The request may come from the patient, or from interested relations, or the doctor himself may have decided that it is the only right and proper thing to do under the circumstances. But it is at the best a most thankless job, apart from the intrinsic difficulties of execution. If the will should cause dissatisfaction, and a family quarrel ensue, which, under the circumstances of stress, is almost sure to be the case, the doctor, however disinterested he may be, and however pure and honest his motive, becomes *ipso facto* a party to the quarrel, and is never forgiven.

What I have done has been raked up and thrown in my teeth years and years afterwards, showing a deep and bitter resentment.

The first will I was brave enough to make was for an old retired farmer of ninety-two, who, like many others, had never made one for fear of immediately fatal consequences.

All his sons and daughters with one exception had married early in life and left him. The exception, a daughter, had kept his house for many years, helped him to save, and nursed him in illness. Quite lately she too had married, her husband taking up his residence in the father's house with them.

It was naturally the old man's strong wish that she should have a double share of his possessions, in return for her long years of devotion. The arrangement seemed to me quite fair under the circumstances, and I drew the will up accordingly. But these excellent brothers and sisters, among them two local preachers, were dreadfully bitter, quarrelled with their sister for life, and with me also. I was abused like a pickpocket up and down dale, and never heard the last of it.

I once disturbed a band of conspirators. Entering a patient's room unexpectedly, I found four of them strenuously holding up the "corpse," while a fifth was directing the dead hand in signature of the will they had just concocted. The "testator" had been dead for four hours.

On another occasion the age on the coffin was younger than the eldest son's age, who as chief mourner was at the head of the funeral procession. This was some cunning scheme to rob the company with whom the "corpse" had been insured. In those days some insurance companies were very slack in their methods, specially when opening up a fresh district. So many industrial policies were allowed by the holders to lapse, that profits accruing from them more than covered any delinquencies of unscrupulous agents.

Funerals or "sidings" as they are regularly called in Yorkshire, are anxiously arranged and provided for, often years beforehand, by the family. How they spread themselves to provide a burying worthy of the station in life of the deceased! If the family had fallen from higher estate, the greater the determination and the pinching. Even the most miserly and mean for once throw prudence to the winds, and have one crowded hour of plenty and extravagance.

Directly after the death of one of my patients I sent the widow a small gift of money. She was nearly destitute, overwhelmed with grief, and worn out with nursing and want of good food. But she had no blinds to draw down in the two front windows of her cottage, and my gift went in the purchase of funeral blinds.

There was rivalry too as to who could go one better in funeral pomp and display. One of Phil May's characters, I believe, remarks, "Wait till we've a funeral at our house, and we'll show yah."

I paid a visit of condolence one day to a bereaved widow, and I found her in great trouble and weeping bitterly. I tried hard to console her with words of comfort, but it was all in vain. Presently I discovered the cause of her woe. Joseph, she was sure, had gone straight to Heaven, but the tiresome butcher from the neighbouring town had forgotten to send the beef ordered for the funeral, and there was no more to be got.

Some forty years ago I was fortunate enough to witness, personally, one of the old-fashioned Yorkshire funerals in all its grandeur. The circumstances were unusually conducive to the display of funeral pomp and fuss, which in those days was considered so necessary to do honour to the dead. The "corpse," Krofer Duffield, was a retired farmer, a well-to-do, hard-bitten Yorkshire-man, known far and wide as a "character." He had always dispensed a bountiful hospitality, and had never been known to run short of good liquor.

It was said, too, that for the last twenty years of his life he had never gone to bed sober. In spite of this he had reached the ripe old age of eighty-six. He was a Roman Catholic, and had been a great sportsman, a combination from which experience taught me to expect the "very best." I was personally "bidden" by a member of the family, in this case his grandson and heir. No wonder when I arrived at the house, shortly after midday, I found a large "company" of relatives and friends assembled to do honour to his memory, and "enjoy" themselves. If they had not enjoyed themselves, I am sure the "corpse" would have been excessively annoyed. Though it was a bitterly cold day in winter, I must personally confess that I thoroughly enjoyed this wonderful ceremony.

Two mutes were stationed on either side of the front door. Each of the bearers had long black silk scarves fixed round their top hats; and to each of the family mourners was presented a pair of black kid gloves.

As the Roman Catholic Church was many miles distant, mourners were treated to a very substantial dinner. Of the rest of us, the "quality" had good old port and sponge cake, and the "many" mulled ale and "parkin" (a Yorkshire variety of gingerbread).

There were many mourning coaches and conveyances of every sort and description.

The director of ceremonies was the family lawyer, who "sorted" us all, and directed who should ride with whom.

In the meantime everybody had taken a last farewell of the deceased in his coffin.

There was of course much delay and confusion, much running about for further refreshments for late arrivals, much getting in and out of carriages, and we were in consequence quite an hour behind scheduled time. However, at last the coffin lid was screwed down, and the gallant old sportsman set off on his last journey across country, beneath the waving and nodding plumes of the hearse.

At the last moment the family lawyer and I were obliged to accommodate two "gentlemen" with evil-smelling clothes, one of whom, with wise forethought for the immediate future, at once proceeded to borrow half a crown from me.

His "Missus," he explained, was so "maddled" in getting him ready for such an important burying, that she had forgotten to give him any ready money. He promised of course to repay me on the first opportunity, but I never saw or smelt him again.

What a strange medley and mix-up of humanity it was. I can see that long straggling procession now as we turned the many winding corners of the distant way. There were top hats of every shape and form, and funeral garments of every cut and fashion, some mouldy with dust, some green with age.

The long tedious journey at last came to an end.

The church was like an ice house, and after the final "siding," we were only too thankful for the hour's rest and warmth arranged for at the three village inns. The journey home was as fast as the horses could make it. A Gargantuan banquet of hot and cold meats was provided on our return, and certainly no funeral feast ever had more ample justice done to it.

The vicar of a large Yorkshire parish was one day accosted on the road by a parishioner, a moor-sider who lived on the distant boundary. Quoth he, "How much do you charge for siding 'em, Parson?" "Ten shillings," replied the parson, "Why do you ask?" "Whya it's like this, Parson. My ole wuman, she is non sa varra capital, and I shall be bringing her along yan o' these days."

Six weeks afterwards the "ole wuman" brought the "ole man" along instead.

An old friend of mine had been offered by the ducal patron a country living, and one day paid a quiet visit of inspection. In the churchyard he found the sexton digging a grave, and introduced himself to him, explaining the purpose of his visit. The sexton was a fine specimen of his order, and after closely scanning my friend, felt very favourably impressed and by way of encouragement remarked, "I have bin sextant here for forty-one years, and I've buried three vicars, and I hope I shall have the honour and pleasure of burying ye."

An old farmer was dying, and the owner of his farm with his wife had walked over the moor to inquire about him and if possible see him. The old housewife who was notoriously mean and miserly, made them a cup of tea, explaining that she was too poor to provide more than simple bread and butter for their entertainment. Unfortunately this was overheard by a grandchild who, childlike, exclaimed, "Oh! grandmother, there's such a beautiful cake in the cupboard." The old woman shouted angrily, "Hod thee noise, doant ye know t'cake's for t'burying."

By way of contrast, I will tell of one pretty little old lady of the moor who was a great friend of mine. She had been a widow many years, living with her two sons and a daughter, in the last farmhouse on one of the moorland roads. She had perfect features and perfect colouring suggestive of dainty Dresden china. She was quite a conversationalist, and had a most retentive memory. I always enjoyed my visits to her. I have no doubt in another sphere of life she would have been a great lady with a fashionable and influential salon.

She was a great favourite with her landlord, a noble lord, who never failed to take a cup of tea with her when he shot that side of the moor.

She was slowly dying from heart disease. The noble lord had asked her what I thought of her condition, and chances of recovery. "Not very favourably, thank your Lordship," she replied. A jolly old Irish peer, standing by and listening, at once chimed in, "My dear good lady, don't you take the slightest notice of what the doctor says on that score. It was twenty years since that three doctors stood round my bedside, like three big ugly black crows, and all three said I hadn't a dog's chance to get better, and would be quite dead by the week was over, and begorra, they're all three dead themselves, everyone of them, and buried, and I have just enjoyed the best day's grouse-shooting I have ever had in my life."

She recounted his cheery and hopeful remarks to me the next day with a twinkle in her eyes, and a little chuckle in her voice. Only a few short weeks afterwards her gentle spirit passed onwards, to my deep regret, the more so because I had been compelled to leave her in the charge of a *locum tenens*, owing to so important an event as my marriage.

Knowing that the end was not far off, I returned from my honeymoon, choosing an indirect route on purpose to introduce my bride to this charming little old lady ; but we were too late, as she had died that morning.

As the only doctor in the district, I was of course morally compelled to attend all these funerals, specially in my earlier days, whatever my feelings or regard for the "corpse" might be. If I had been in any way remiss in this duty I should have been considered to fall short of the high ideal of perfection to which a country doctor should attain, and any shortcomings in attendance or treatment of the deceased would not have been condoned.

A country doctor I knew made a terrible error in his diagnosis of a case. He told the relations of a man who had taken to his bed that his ailment was one of downright bone laziness, and ordered them to get him up and out for a walk. However, while they were nagging at him to get up and assisting him to dress, he gave up the ghost.

Needless to say this shook their faith in their family doctor to the very foundation, but the arrival of a magnificent wreath from the doctor on the day of the funeral—and magnificent wreaths are rare at these moorland funerals — rapidly restored him to favour again.

I cannot say I did not enjoy some of these "sidings." Many of my best stories I gleaned, after the disposal of the "corpse" and the ham.

It was very interesting to see variations in funeral rites and ceremony, specially as old customs are slowly dying out. My appreciation of the humorous helped me through what to others would have been often a dull time.

Sometimes I had the greatest difficulty in preserving an appropriately solemn and sedate expression. For instance, on one occasion the local minister began his funeral oration over the deceased, who had been abnormally stout, and for many months confined to bed, by saying, "Brother Layfield dwelt very largely in bed." Was it a joke to cheer us up or not? The precept *de mortuis nil nisi bonum* was sometimes very liberally interpreted. Rogues and rascals were for the nonce transformed into paragons and saints. They would positively have blushed if they had heard their own funeral orations.

An artist once wandered into a remote Yorkshire dale, to him till then quite an unknown land, in search of suitable quarters for six months' hard work. Eventually after much inquiry he found an ideal place. The people were kind, the food good and well cooked, the rooms most comfortable, the air very bracing, and the country round extremely beautiful. Moreover, near at hand was a picturesque lake, situated in a thick wood, with a rich growth of rushes, iris, and many water plants, just the ideal setting and inspiration for a subject he had long contemplated, "Moses in the Bulrushes."

In these congenial surroundings he worked well and rapidly, and when the six months had quickly passed, was more than satisfied with what he had accomplished.

That great work, and afterwards historic painting, "Moses in the Bulrushes," was completed to his own critical and complete satisfaction.

Almost from the beginning his relations with the natives had been most cordial. At first they naturally regarded with some suspicion the first "painting chap" they had ever seen, but this had soon passed away. They became interested in his work, and even ventured to criticise it, though of course always favourably. Gifts of pipefuls of tobacco now and again cemented the friendly feeling.

Before his departure he decided to invite all his new friends to an "at home" and private view of his sketches, landscapes, and *magnum opus*.

When the evening arrived his friends, without exception, turned up. There was a splendid light, and a generous supply of good ale, tobacco, and light refreshments.

"Moses in the Bulrushes" of course occupied the place of honour.

Among his guests was the great man of the place, the largest farmer and the richest man within miles. He was a big heavy man, with a huge red beard, and very hearty jovial manner. To him the artist naturally paid special attention, taking him by the arm and explaining each sketch and painting in detail.

The farmer's praise of the work was sincere, generous, and unstinted, his only difficulty being the limited supply of appropriate adjectives in his vocabulary to express adequately his intense admiration.

The climax was reached when he stood in awe-struck contemplation of the immortal work. So great was his astonishment, that he could only remark, "Why, this caps owt! By gum it deeas." Then critically examining Moses, "So that's little Moses? It's loikely he's bin dead a sight o' years. Wha long, think ye?" "Oh," replied the artist, "about three thousand years."

"Three thousand years," gasped the farmer, "and ye've painted 'im real arter three thousand years?"

"Yes," modestly answered the artist.

"I tell 'ee what it be. Yah's yan o' t'cleverest fellahs oi've ever set ees on." Then followed a long pause, at last broken by the farmer.

"I wish ye'd coom an' pent me faither."

There was some hesitation on the artist's part, arising not from disinclination, but from the fact that he had arranged to leave as soon as his canvases could be packed.

The farmer, misunderstanding, and thinking his hesitation was due to a question of payment, at once said, "Ah'll pay ye roight eneeaf. T'brass is all roight, ise nut er'yarpenny chap. Hoo much a foot de ye charge?"

"It's not a question," protested the artist, "of payment at all. I shall only be too pleased to do what I possibly can, in return for the kindness I have received from everybody. I had arranged to leave at once, but after all a couple of days will make little difference. I will come down to-morrow afternoon, if you will have the old gentleman ready in his best clothes."

"'Ave t'aud gentleman ready!" replied the farmer, as if he had not heard aright. "Wya he's bin dead fowty years or mair."

"Then it will be impossible for me to paint him if he is dead."

"Ye carnt pent 'im when 'ees only bin dead fowty year! And ye've pented Moses wha's dead three thousand years?"

This deduction was unanswerable.

"Have you a photograph or any picture of him?" asked the artist.

"Nay, we've nae pictur, but he war varra loike me at my time o' loife. Onnyways yah mun deea t'best ye can."

So the artist went to the old kitchen of the farmhouse, and made all possible use of the setting of old furniture, and all details he could glean. He worked hard, galvanised into lifelike existence the old dog from his skin on the kitchen floor, and by much skill and imagination succeeded in reproducing what he thought might have some possible resemblance to the old gentleman.

It was really a marvellous achievement, perhaps even greater than that of "Moses in the Bulrushes."

When at last the farmer was brought in to inspect the result of the artist's strenuous labours, he was nearly speechless with astonishment at the wondrous power of the artist's brush.

"By gum, this knocks t'stuffin' out o' Moses in t'bulrushes. It deeas an' all. There's t'aud dog Rover, t'aud armchair, t'aud clock, t'aud dresser, t'aud chetch-wardener pipe, and 'is sup o' gin an' watter."

Then after a long and searching scrutiny of his dead parent's features, he remarked rather sadly, "Aye, but he has altered!"

A newly appointed vicar noticed that there was no regular footpath to the vestry door, but only a narrow track zigzagging between the tomb-stones.   Immediately to remove the historic stones would not of course have been permitted under any circumstances, but little by little the vicar and his faithful coadjutor, the sexton, began to move them a few inches at a time to either side. It was done so gradually that nobody noticed it, nor was anybody in the secret.   At the end of eight years the vicar pointed out to the annual vestry that it would be advisable to make a regular footpath, where there was such an evident space. After inspection the plan was passed, carried, and, within a few days, completed.   Then of course two or three old Methusalehs came poking round, commenting that it was all "varra queer," and threatening all sorts of inquiry and trouble which never came.

One winter's evening, after a long and arduous day's work, I was informed that there was a man waiting to see me in the stable-yard.   I found it was "Lovely John."   Why Lovely? Was he not the ugliest man in the ghyll? Years ago, it appears, that even he had had some feelings of romance hidden somewhere under his tough hide, and in concluding a *billet doux* to some fair maid of the moor to whom he had given his heart, had signed himself "your Lovely John."   And the name had stuck.

"Happen," he said, "you'll be coming up ower yonder," jerking his finger over his shoulder in the direction of his moorland home, "to-morn or the day after.   Maybe ye would call and see my missus, she's killed wi' pain in her innards."   I said it was quite possible, and should come.

“Maybe,” he added, “you would mak. her a bottle to tak wi’ me, and put her to rights in no time.”

On further questioning I gathered that his wife’s condition was much more serious than he had led me to infer. I said I would walk up quietly the three miles odd, and see her, to which suggestion he agreed and left me to follow on.

I must explain the setting of this strange story. This man, his brother, and wife lived alone together. He owned his farm, which was quite a good one, and both he and his brother had saved a substantial sum in addition. But they were notoriously mean and miserly.

The house was comfortless, there were no carpets on the floors, and they had only the barest necessities with which to carry on a fair-sized farm. The wife was the worst of the three. Meanness and miserliness were second nature to her, and were bred in her bones. Only a few days after her death, her father and mother came to demand back the dowry of £100 which they had given her twenty-five years before.

The only exception to this atmosphere of meanness was that Lovely John loved good ale and whisky, could not pass any inn without wetting his whistle, and on market days usually returned home “market fresh.”

When I arrived, I found the woman’s condition quite as bad or worse than I expected, and wondered how she had endured the dreadful pain for several days. I explained that an immediate operation was necessary to save her life, and even then it was probably too late.

I asked Lovely John to get on his horse and ride as fast as the wind to the nearest country town with a request for a doctor there to come out at once to my assistance.

"It's maybe not so bad as that. Maybe it would do to-morn, market day," he remarked.

"No, you must go at once, as fast as possible," I replied.

"It's none a gallopin' matter?" he asked.

"It is a galloping matter, off you go, ride like Jehu." I then went to the farm-buildings to look for the brother. I found him and asked him to fetch the woman's mother, and a farmer's wife I knew, a very handy woman and quite reliable in matters of this sort.

"It's none a gallopin' matter?" he asked. It seemed galloping was quite a family adjective.

"Yes," I said, "gallop away and bring them as soon as you can, because I must go home soon to get my operation instruments together."

Then I went upstairs again to talk to the patient, and prepare her for the coming ordeal. I explained I had sent her husband off to Muxley to fetch another doctor, and her brother to fetch her mother and Mrs Peacock. I stayed chatting with her some little time when I heard some sounds, in what I thought was an empty kitchen below, which I proceeded immediately to investigate.

Judge of my surprise when I discovered the cause of the noise was Lovely John shaving in a most painstaking and laborious way.

"What the devil are you doing here shaving? I thought you were miles on your way to Muxley," I said very angrily.

"I never go to Muxley without shaving. Besides it's market day to-morn," was his reply.

"Shaving be damned, get off at once."

"It's none a gallopin' matter is it?"

"Yes. Gallop like blazes."

I saw him off at last, and heard him gallop into the night, then rejoined the patient. Then again I heard more noises, which further investigation proved to be the brother in the dairy very busily skimming the milk, and packing the butter for market by the light of a stable lantern.

"What the devil are you doing there, too?" I asked. "I thought you were at the end of the ghyll by now, fetching Mrs Peacock and Mrs Taylor. Now hurry off."

"It's none a gallopin' matter?"

"Yes," I replied, now very angry. "Gallop like Hell, but don't break your neck."

Not till I heard him galloping up the moorland road was I satisfied that these barbarians were well away on their respective errands.

I then returned to the woman, and found her in darkness. The last candle in the farmhouse had burnt out. I searched everywhere for a light of some sort, but in vain, made up the fire, and reluctantly left the suffering woman alone in that lonely farmhouse. I explained that I must get home as soon as possible to meet the other doctor, but she made not the slightest demur, and seemed quite happy about being left by herself.

I walked thoughtfully home. On passing the village inn, close to my house, judge of my fury when I heard the raucous voice of Lovely John bidding good-night to the landlord, as he was mounting his horse.

My language became far too lurid for the pages of even this truthful narrative.

To my enquiry why he was not returning from Muxley, rather than just setting off after all my urgings, he shouted, "I never goes to Muxley without calling for a sup at Danby. It's none a gallopin' matter surely."

I was so sick and weary now of galloping matters that I hurried away and left him.

When after all these delays my colleague and I arrived eventually at the patient's bedside, it was too late, all her pain had gone, and gangrene had supervened.

On hearing the verdict she was least disturbed of any of us, and took it all with stoical resignation. She shook hands with us, and hoped we should all meet in Heaven.

Her sole remaining anxiety then was to hear that the market butter was ready packed, to say good-bye to her only friend, and sell her her last marketable ducks.

So the brother was again hurried off on horse-back to the far end of another ghyll, and even he now realised that it was a galloping matter after all.

Lovely John received my grave opinion, too, very quietly. "She's been a good wife to me," he said. "She war a rare butter maker, and she's helped me to put some brass together, but she war varra mean about a sup of out to drink. Onyways she shall have as good a siding as need be. But it's a bad job for me. How can I deea without a wife. Maybe ye know of a likely yan, Doctor. Keep yer ees open." This before his wife was dead.

True to his promise, John gave her a funeral well up to the best traditions of the ghyll. Good Yorkshire ham, good ale and liquor, and funeral baked meats in plenty for all those bidden. He insisted on black streamers to his hat and looked a weird scarecrow of a mourner.

His final remark on alighting at the church gate from the funeral coach was characteristic. "My word, it's grand and comfortable riding in a trap like yon—I could ride all t'day in it."

There was a large "company" assembled. Not a tear dropped, nor was there any sign of emotion beyond a dreadful contortion of Lovely John's face before he gave up the hopeless effort of squeezing out a tear.

"Mrs Buck bids you to Mr Buck's funeral at two o'clock on Friday, at the Carr House Farm," was the style of the customary bidding. The bidder on this occasion would be Mrs Buck's son, or some near male relative. Rarely a great family friend would undertake this duty. This ceremonial bidding implied that you would be expected punctually at the house, where you might possibly join in a private family service held in the best parlour, or if this was not large enough in the house kitchen. These services at the house were not by any means universal, but were very frequent; more so perhaps at Chapel than Church buryings. The service would be conducted by the Church or Chapel minister, and a hymn would be always sung. I was once present at such a service in the drawing-room of a large Yorkshire mansion where a member of an old county family had died. The service concluded, port or sherry or home-made wine would be handed round with sponge cake or biscuits. Then followed the procession to the church. At the conclusion of the Church or Chapel service you were expected to return to the house to do full justice to the "ham" and funeral meats.

At the purely moorland funerals a hearse was not always used, but the coffin carried by six bearers, who often would be of the same sex or description as the "corpse." Six married women would carry a married woman, six maidens a maiden, six boy or girl children, a boy or girl child, and six single men a single man. The carrying in these cases was always by hand, by means of long towels, and never on the shoulders. Over the snow a hand sledge would be dragged. The way of the procession would naturally be the shortest possible one. When the moorland church was some distance away by road, lane, bridle-path or footpath, rests or halts by the way would be taken at intervals and hymns sung.

There is a well-established belief that whichever way a corpse is carried, "the corpse way," that road thereby and thereafter becomes constituted a public right of way; I am told that in strict English law this does not hold. I know, however, it was acted on in good faith on the moorlands. In one case in my practice a death had occurred at a farmhouse within the precincts of the large private park of a county mansion. There was the ordinary right of way to the farmhouse, but for the funeral procession to have followed this would have involved a very long, irksome, and inconvenient détour to the moorland church. The privilege of a much shorter way through the park was applied for and granted on payment of a small acknowledgment.

The boundary line between two parishes in my practice ran obliquely through a farmhouse, and the question once arose as to which parish churchyard should be the burial-place of a man who had died there. The bed on which he lay was in both parishes, and the deciding point was the position of the corpse's head.

By far the largest country funeral I ever attended was that of a cattle dealer, who was barely forty years of age. Cattle dealers are anything but popular characters on the moorside. I have heard the bitterest and most venomous things said even about the best of them. They drive such hard bargains, and farmers have such long memories and never forget or forgive sales made under duress. Like doctors and policemen, they are tolerated as necessary evils. It speaks much for the high character and fine personality of this man that his funeral was attended by farmers from the valleys and fells of Cumberland, Westmoreland, and other distant places. The aspect of the village was like a fair day, yet all were hospitably and generously entertained. The oldest inhabitant could not recall the like of such a burying.

The father of this man was the Nestor and most successful of all the dealers, and was known as the relieving officer of the farmers; and, although he had a far-flung connection, he carried all his reckonings and lendings in his head. Many of these old cattle dealers did the same. They were ready reckoners and never by any chance made a mistake. This man's opportunity came in those terribly dark days of the cattle plague or rinderpest, and he got the last ounce out of it. Farmers by the hundred were ruined, and many insurance companies collapsed. The North Riding markets were closed, and in consequence the farmers were at their wits' end to raise liquid capital. In the West Riding the cattle could only be removed under a magistrate's order. Fortunately he lived near the boundary of the Ridings in a remote village, and the Squire, and local magistrate there, who farmed his own land extensively, was very sympathetic and appreciative of difficulties. He had a conveniently deaf ear and blind eye, and could always be relied upon to sign an order. The dealer described very graphically to me in later years his doings in those stirring days. Often he rode a hundred miles a day on horses borrowed, hired, or bought. Drovers went about disguised as women. Cattle were smuggled across the boundary in a most ingenious and daring fashion. They were swum across the river, or driven across the moorland at dead of night.

When, by rare good luck and hard work, a cattle dealer was able to put together, as this man had done, any considerable capital, he had a tremendous pull as a lending dealer, specially in those precarious times. Hence his sobriquet of the farmers' relieving officer. The majority of cattle dealers I know did badly and generally failed sooner or later. There is a saying that cattle dealers live well and die poor. The really successful ones could be counted on one hand. The clever buyer and judge of beasts is like the poet, born, not made. I always knew when the markets were rising, by seeing these fellows galloping furiously over the country.

The original parish of the old mother church had been very extensive, in one direction being quite eighteen miles across, and even after daughter churches had one by one been built, many of the inhabitants of the remote villages preferred to be buried in the old churchyard. A very old man used to describe to me some of these funerals. Some were so late in the day that the final interment was by lamplight, or even by the flickering light of a candle. In some cases the funeral parties were snowed up on the moorlands. Very often when the way was inordinately long the funeral party would stay at least one night at the village inn, and in some cases two nights, holding high feast and drinking heavily.

In November 1902 a funeral party of one coach with the hearse came fifty miles over the rough high moorland roads. The time of interment had been arranged for two o'clock in the afternoon, but it was seven o'clock before the moorland church was at length reached, and the actual interment could only be accomplished with the light from stable lanterns. It poured with rain the whole of the tedious journey. In one place it was necessary to negotiate the descent of a very long steep hill. The horses were quite unequal to the strain, and the drivers went some miles forward on foot till they could procure some old shoes wherewith to reinforce the brakes.

At one resting-place an old Yorkshire woman quoted to one of the five mourners the old Yorkshire saying :—

> "Blessed is t'bride that t'sun shines on,
> An' blessed is t'deead that t'rain rains on."

In one of our nearest dales the local doctor's wife, in her husband's absence, attended the funeral of an old patient, a woman, who was a member of that very rare sect, the followers of Joanna Southcote, of whom there were a few in that village. Never having been present at any of their services or funerals, she was full of anticipatory interest. The officiating member of the flock was the local butcher, who appeared adorned in his ordinary blue working smock, the other members of the sect also wearing their everyday apparel. There was no ritual or service. When the coffin had been lowered into the grave, the butcher, standing at the head of the grave, gazed very steadily down at the coffin for some minutes before delivering what the doctor's wife thought would be a funeral oration, but which consisted simply of these words, "Ah think they mun (might) have laid her a bit straighter." Evidently the angle of the grave or the coffin within offended his sense of the rectilineal.

CHAPTER IX

SOME CURIOUS CASES

KIT BALDERSTONE, though he occasionally got very tipsy, was no afternoon farmer, but following the example and tradition of his father and grandfathers, industriously and strenuously wooed and cherished into smiling cultivation the rough moorland allotments of his farm. There is a Spanish proverb, "*El pie del dueno estierco para la heredad,*" which means that the farmer's foot is the best manure for the farm. Now this man's feet were always moving and his activity was richly rewarded.

Owing to his unfortunate lapses from sobriety he had three most severe accidents within two years, any one of which might easily have been fatal; but with the happy luck which so often befriends the drunken, and his stout heart of oak, he made marvellous recoveries. One of these was so dramatic, and brought me quite early in my practice such a great local reputation, that I cannot refrain from describing it : moreover, it is of unusual medical interest, one similar case being described in Sir Eric Erichsen's classical work on Surgery. This "miraklous man" would generally return from the weekly local market very late and decidedly "market fresh." On one occasion when he was later than usual, his anxious wife at last heard the horse and cart stop opposite the farmhouse, and on going out to "threeap" or scold him, was surprised to find the cart empty. As he did not appear after some minutes, she called her sons to unyoke and help her to search for him. It was a pitch dark night. On the farmhouse road were several successive gates, which were usually open, with the exception of the last one opening on to the main moorland road, which was kept closed. Here they found him on the ground, nearly unconscious, and groaning in intense agony. He had evidently been badly crushed between the "steean steeap of the yat" and the cart-wheel of his cart in opening the gate. With the help of neighbours he was first carried into the farmhouse kitchen, and then with much difficulty up the narrow stairs to his bedroom. No sooner was he deposited there than, as his wife described it, he began to "swell up awl ower." The urgent message I received merely stated that "Kit Balderstone was fair bruzzen wi' wind an' swellin' up fast." Thinking it was a case of acute dyspepsia I arrived at the farm without any surgical appliances. On the bed I found my friend looking for all the world like a blue balloon. It was as if somebody had used a force pump and inflated him. What had evidently happened was that he had broken some ribs, and in carrying him upstairs the sharp edge of one or two had been forced through not only the pleural membranes but the lung tissue itself, producing a valve-like opening in the latter. With each inspiration air was being drawn through the lungs into the pleural cavity, and then with the recoil of expiration, forced into the areolar spaces of the true skin, producing what is known as surgical emphysema. How these spaces intercommunicate over the whole body was realistically illustrated by this graphic case. They make possible the process of flaying in all animals. He was just conscious, cyanosed, gasping for breath, and already the air had penetrated as far as the eyelids, completely closing the eyes, and to the backs of the hands and feet. He was a hard human air-cushion, and the air was surely squeezing the life out of him. Over his back it appeared to be at least six inches deep. Fortunately I had a very fast trotter, able, when put to it, to do seventeen miles an hour, and I raced home for a trocar with which to tap this air-cushion. On my return the grief-stricken wife greeted me with the words, "Ye're ower laate; it's awl owered an' he's geean. T'lads have geean for Mrs Feasby an' Mrs Hannen to lay 'im out." When I arrived at the bedside I was fortunately in time to see the very faintest effort of respiration, or to use a realistic Yorkshire term for dying, "It war t'last fetch." I immediately plunged the instrument into the cushion first on one side and then on the other, and, following an audible escape of air in each instance, had the supreme satisfaction of seeing an immediate return of respiration and in ten minutes of consciousness. In the meantime the two ladies or "pinkers," as they are still called on the moors, arrived on the scene with mixed feelings of disappointment that there was no job for them and of joy at the miracle that had been accomplished. There was hæmorrhage from the lung for at least a fortnight following the accident, and so much damage had been done on both sides, that I was never able to apply even a bandage or strapping.   The most delicate examination showed that many ribs had been broken in both chests.   It was seven days before the patient had the slightest vision.   If for the time being I had achieved a local Homeric reputation, my patient became equally famous as "the man who was deead yance bud cam back to life ageean." Any reference to the next world in this man's presence even to-day is followed by a remark of this kind, "Thou knows awl abart it o' course, thou's bin deead yance."   What eloquent testimony to the *vis medicatrix Naturæ* in his case, for he made a perfect recovery.   An enthusiastic and admiring neighbour who often describes this eventful night, always ends her description with, "My! t'doctor's grand Galloway war a clipper to go."

If there is one great thing that some of us can thank Almighty God for during our pilgrimage through life, it is the faithful love and devotion of our dog and horse friends.   It is one of Nature's greatest masterpieces and choicest gifts, and the thought or doubt that they may not perhaps accompany us across the Great Divide seems to deaden the instinct for belief in a life hereafter. More constant than that of human friends, it is a sunbeam which lights up the clouds of our darkest hours, and guards us from despair.   This mare in the day when carriage lamps were not compulsory, never made a mistake, but brought me home safely many hundred of miles through the darkest and foggiest of nights.   She had racing blood in her, and was so mettlesome that we were always compelled when away from home to yoke her with her head away, yet in the stable she was as gentle as a lamb. I pensioned her off to end her days with a kindly farmer, and years afterwards, whenever I paid her a visit, I never failed to receive her welcoming whinny as she trotted to me across her pasture.

I have frequently come across cases of men, who, while admirably energetic and industrious in their own occupation or business, seemed absolutely incapable of resisting the impulse at almost regular intervals to indulge in a drunken carouse. They would then throw all prudence and wisdom to the winds, except as regards their own special business or occupation. As an example—I knew one very wealthy and successful manufacturer who had these regular attacks, and regardless of expense or publicity would rush about from inn to inn, followed by a band of human leeches and parasites, whom under ordinary circumstances he would have contemptuously ignored, but now treated with more than friendly tolerance. It was most interesting to note though, that should any attempt be made in a matter of business to take advantage of his condition to drive an unfavourable bargain, however drunk he was, his native acumen and grit were all there, and it was an impossibility to corner him. The mentality or causation of these attacks it is most difficult to explain satisfactorily. It would seem that civilised man occasionally kicks instinctively against all order and restraint, and feels now and again a primitive and irresistible longing to let himself go. Some, even, in response to inquiry would assure me that they felt all the better in health for these bouts afterwards. It is well known that the upset of the human body by sea-sickness is often followed by an improvement in health, and so possibly a drunken upset may produce the same result. One well-known local preacher, then a quite reformed character, once confessed to me that he occasionally actually longed for a two or three days' debauch, explaining that in former unregenerate days he felt so much better after one, both in body and mind.

The following two incidents illustrate the influence and power of suggestion. One of my South Yorkshire patients was a file-cutter, who brought his supply of files to be cut to his moorland cottage, and was paid by piece-work. He was a victim of lead poisoning from absorption from the lead moulds in which the files are placed. Lead poisoning is a matter of personal idiosyncrasy. Some, who disregard every precaution, never suffer in the slighest degree from it, while others even after most scrupulous care are compelled to cease all contact with lead or its compounds. This man who was an expert workman had developed paralysis of the extensor muscle of the hand and finger, known as "wrist drop," and it was a bad case. A physician, who had seen him, prescribed small doses of strychnine which I made up for him in pill form. He improved very rapidly under this treatment, so much so that, thinking he could not have too much of a good thing, he commenced taking, in spite of careful warning, at first twice then thrice the dose. He early recognised the physiological effects of the drug by his involuntary muscular twitchings, and soon therefore began designating his pills as his "jumping pills." I have no doubt suggestion contributed to rendering his jumping efforts more violent. However, he took his pills so recklessly, and his jumping performances became so alarming, that I became afraid he would take a sudden leap into eternity, and therefore determined to avoid any cumulation by making his pills up for a few weeks minus strychnine. After taking these harmless pills for about a fortnight he came to me, looking terribly severe, and very important. "Noo, Doctor, did thou mak them last lot o' pills up yersen?" he asked. "Yes," I replied. "Thou's sure?" "Yes, perfectly." "Well, there's summat wrong, t'missus gav me yan (one) last neet an' I hadn't bin i' bed five minutes afore I jumped clean out o' bed and nearly through t'window."

Influenza spread sometimes so rapidly, specially on the exposed tablelands, that I am perfectly certain climatic influences played a much greater part in its causation than personal contagion. Whole households of many adjacent farms would simultaneously be rendered so suddenly helpless, that the stock could not be fed or the cows milked. This observation coincides with similar ones that have been made in other parts of the world. I was once called to visit a moorland farmer during such an epidemic. I put the thermometer in the old man's armpit, asked him the usual routine of questions, gave the ordinary directions, and went away quite forgetful of the thermometer. I only made the discovery that I had left it at the next call quite three miles away, when it was too late to retrieve it. I expected it would be hopelessly smashed. What a welcome I got from the old fellow the next day. "Aye, Bairnie, Ah's glad to see thee I can tell thee, bud what a job I've had wi' yer fanglement. It kept slippin' doon an' I puts it back an' it slipped ageean, an' I puts it back ageean. By gum I nobbut winked (slept) a bit afore it slipt ageean. I tewed all t'neet wi' it, bud it's deean me ner hurt (much good), an' I sall soon be makin' good mends." There at any rate was my precious instrument quite whole. I did not enlighten him about my forgetfulness, but left him with the impression that though modern "fanglements" might be troublesome they were effective.

I once explained as I thought very carefully to a wife how to iron her husband's back over brown paper, an excellent treatment for lumbago, from which he was at the time suffering. Instead of finding him much relieved by it, I found him just as amiable as a sore bear. In fact he was sorer than the bear. The woman, it appeared, had first ironed the paper and then given the luckless back a hard scrubbing, making it nearly red raw. As she was not a very amiable lady and a notorious threeaper, I rather suspect she had taken advantage of the opportunity to pay off old scores.

In the old days before the binaural stethoscope superseded the old wooden trumpet-like stethoscope, I was called out of bed to see a patient who was suffering from asthma. I had seen him the previous day and had sounded and thumped his chest very thoroughly. After delivering the message, the messenger said, "Mind thou brings thy thumper, t'thumping and t'braying thou gav him did him a seet o' good."

I had not used for very long my first binaural stethoscope, of which I was inordinately proud, and which I always wore in a conspicuous position in my front coat pocket, when a very old Yorkshire woman, living high up on the moors, took me gently aside and said, "I deeant hod wi' yer waring yer midwifery concarns so as t'men foak can see 'em, it's noan ser nice for t'puir bodies as has ter hav 'em." (I don't agree with your carrying your midwifery instruments about so that the men can see them, it's not very nice for the poor bodies who will be obliged to have them.) Till then I had not realised that my up-to-date stethoscope might be so regarded, and I took the old lady's kindly hint.

CHAPTER X

INSANITY

STATISTICS show that the incidence of insanity in sparsely populated country and moorland districts is above the average. In reality it is much higher than would appear from the figures. There are many in the country, living the lives of ordinary people in perfect freedom and under no restraint, who, under the official and stricter surveillance of the town, would be locked up at once. They are looked upon as harmless; everybody knows them, humours their madness, and makes due allowance for their vagaries.

Then there are many more on the borderland, half-cracked and half-baked beings who, if exposed to the strain and excitement of town life, would break down at once. Occasionally, of course, a tragedy does occur, just as one day the passer-by on the public footpath is gored to death by the reputedly quiet and harmless bull.

These mad folk marry and intermarry and propagate children, and so multiply the evil. Fortunately, by a compensating law of nature, there is ever a strong tendency in the offspring to revert to normal type; these marriages, more-over, are frequently childless, or, if not childless, productive of weaklings who die early in life.

It was my duty as a poor-law medical officer to certify all those who, by their inability to pay the higher charges of a private asylum, became *ipso facto* paupers, and if I had certified all those I considered to be insane I should have locked up a big proportion of the country-side.

It was said by a great authority, Maudsley, I think, that it was the half-cracked relations of the insane who hindered the proper treatment of them under restraint. How they used to lie to me when I asked the pertinent question whether there was any insanity in the family. I was once certifying a farmer whose relations swore stoutly to the contrary, yet I knew quite well that one of his brothers had murdered a sister under peculiarly atrocious circumstances, and was at that moment confined in a criminal asylum.

Consanguinity in marriage is a great factor in the causation of insanity, and these moorland people intermarried so much that the maze of relationship was more than bewildering. One never knew where it began or where it ended. Nieces were sisters-in-law, brothers-in-law were stepsons, and so on. I felt I was going mad myself in threading my way through this labyrinth of relationship. I was for ever discovering new complications.

Another great factor is the extreme monotony of their lives. Man is essentially a sociable animal, and solitary confinement often means a punishment worse than death. These moorland dwellers love their lonely homes, are loth to leave them, and, like their sheep, are eager to return to them, but this very loneliness and isolation renders them more liable to collapse under any sudden shock, strain, or mental excitement. One could see the effect of the religious revivals in the many cases of nervous collapse and actual insanity which followed.

Finally, a good deal of hard drinking goes on, and much of it is perforce of the secret kind. The secret drinker is always the worst to cure, and that is why, apart from other reasons, women, when they are drinkers, are more hopeless than men. Some of these cases, directly due to drink, were the most dangerous I had to deal with, and yet under restraint were the most easily cured.

Without, I hope, wearying the reader, I am tempted here briefly to correct certain misconceptions in the popular mind with regard to madness. It is naturally quite easy to recognise madness when the victim is raving maniacally, or is deeply melancholic and refusing food. It is in dealing with one who is of quiet demeanour, and behaves to all outward appearances like a rational being, but has a fixed delusion, often a most dangerous one, that the difficulty arises. He knows that he is considered by his relations and friends to be mad, and that they regard as a delusion what he is firmly convinced to be the most important of truths. He meets with so much contradiction on the point that he cunningly conceals his delusion (and will even for the nonce affect to be free of it) in order to gain his own ends.

It takes the wind out of one's sails when a patient greets one, as I have been greeted, with the words, "Now I know what you have come for, you wish to send me to the asylum." Weary hours I have spent with this class of case, and not without some personal risk. It is only when a little excited or perhaps when his patience has been worn out by incessant questioning, that the monomaniac suddenly throws off his cunning caution and lets himself go, laying bare his delusion in all its nakedness.

With regard to this fixed delusion I was helped to appreciate the madman's point of view by a little incident which once happened to me. I was returning late one beautiful calm and moonlight night from a moorland vicarage where I had been spending the evening, when, passing over the edge of a deep ghyll, I suddenly felt a violent tremor of the earth, which lasted some twenty seconds. There was no railway within miles to account for such a remarkable tremor. On reaching my home some miles away, I met the village policeman and at once asked him if he had noticed it. He said he had not, and seemed much surprised at my question. The next day I made the same inquiry of my friends and patients with the same result. In fact nobody believed a word of my story. Finding myself alone in my belief, I began to doubt the evidence of my own senses. However, two days afterwards, the daily papers reported the occurrence of a slight earthquake shock at the time in question in the western counties, with earth tremors extending to the north through the hilly districts of Yorkshire and Lancashire. Imagine how pleased I was to read this corroboration. Without it I should in all probability have come to believe in course of time that I had been the victim of an hallucination.

The moods or degree of madness of these crazy folk used to vary considerably. Some days they were astonishingly tractable and amenable to reason, while on other days they were ready for any devilry or mischief—changes of course firmly believed by the country folk to be due to the moon's influence, but really due to the variation in blood-pressure.

One of these moonstruck creatures had already been in an asylum once for a short time, and the story went about that on this occasion, when he arrived with a half-baked relation of the same name at the institution, the doctors had been in so much doubt as to which was the lunatic, that they nearly succeeded in locking up the wrong man. There is no need to describe his appearance, beyond stating that he was the exact facsimile of Uncle Sam Slick with his long goatee beard. He was the terror of a small hamlet in the middle of the moorland, consisting of two or three farms, seven or eight cottages, and a chapel, and in particular of his faithful wife, who was of course a cousin. He kept a small store, played the harmonium at the chapel, had five children, and £500 in the bank. I was very sorry for his wife, and most reluctant to put him under restraint, because I knew the £500 would soon melt in asylum charges. More-over, I was by no means sure he was really mad. He puzzled me very much and gave me a good deal of trouble. At times when he was excited by a full moon and unusually naughty, I would, as a measure of precaution, have him carefully watched by his neighbours. Against one of these he nursed a small private grievance. One day this man and

another farmer were sitting quietly by him, when
he suddenly struck a most vicious blow at the
obnoxious neighbour, which missed its mark and
landed heavily on the stomach of the other man—
winding him, and nearly finishing him off. He
apologised most profusely to the latter, explaining
that he had intended the blow for his companion.
There was too much method here, I thought.

To frighten his wife he used to rush furiously
at the sides of bacon hung up in his kitchen, with
a big carving knife, stabbing them all over.

Late one Sunday night the station-master of
the little country town, a local preacher, came to
me to demand the man's immediate incarceration.
At the afternoon's service, while playing the second
hymn, he had been so carried away with religious
ecstasy and musical emotion that he continued to
sing at the top of his voice, playing magnificent
chords the while and rolling his body from side to
side. Goodness knows how long he would have
continued at this little game, for he was a tough
old bird, had not a member of the congregation
pluckily pulled him off his perch. When the third
hymn came, he returned quietly to the instrument
and gave no further trouble. He entertained the
station-master afterwards to tea, and finding that
he was getting the worst of it in a theological
argument on the subject of the Unjust Steward,
had seized him by the throat and given him a
terrible shaking.

On another occasion he got up in the middle of
the night, and after very quietly dressing, got the
carving knife and narrowly scrutinised his wife's
face to see if she were asleep. Satisfied on this

point, he carefully packed in a butter basket the best china tea-service, carried it a mile on to the moor and then unpacked it, leaving it among the heather covered with bracken.

His wife had cautiously followed at a distance to watch his proceedings, and a few days afterwards, when the moon had passed the quarter, brought back the tea-service, and restored it to its proper place without comment from her spouse.

On another occasion I made him walk some part of the distance home with me, giving him all the time a severe admonishing on his wickedness. On his return, his wife told me, he got two long yule candles, lighted them, brought down the family Bible, opened it at the "Song of Solomon," and therefrom read aloud to his wife till far into the morning.

Finally, one day he took off every rag of clothing, and in stark nakedness and in anything but his right mind, attended to the demands of his customers, to their great consternation. I am sure they sought in vain for the human form divine in his scarecrow of a body. Although it was very hot weather, there was no excuse for this kind of behaviour; so I had him put under lock and key again.

One of my patients, whom I will call Mrs Buckton, was a good-looking and well-made widow woman of thirty-eight years of age. She was a native of the district, but had left it when she was about eighteen for South Lancashire, where she had married, and had had two children, Bobby and Jacky, now aged eleven and fifteen. She lived in a picturesque, well-built, if somewhat lonely cottage, in one of our numerous ghylls. She was undoubtedly mad, but I was never asked to certify her, nor did I feel inclined to do so.

Her fixed delusion, and apparently her only one, was that she was persecuted and tormented by a demon of a man who never desisted from his obnoxious attentions. These attentions she described to me as consisting of horrible grimacings, fixing her with a malignant eye, uttering dreadful noises with his mouth, laughing, snorting, hissing, and groaning.

I never heard or saw anything of course, but it was evidently very real to her.

Her persecutor never for a moment left her precincts. In the night he was in the chimney of her bedroom, in the daytime on the roof of the cottage, or sitting astride the sides of bacon in the dimly lighted kitchen, or lurking behind bushes in the garden, or in any convenient hole or corner into which he could creep.

Whenever she went out for a walk he invariably followed, sneaking behind hedges, and never ceasing to emit his horrible noises.

She was only safe when she went to church or chapel; her devil, it appears, was then out-deviled by the squeaking devil, as the organ is still called in country places. Her regular attendance earned her high commendation from the parson and the minister.

She led a lonely life, save for the company of her two boys. She had quarrelled with all her friends, because they refused to believe in the existence of this persecuting monster.

She suffered occasionally from minor ailments,

and invariably called me in. On all these occasions
the procedure was the same. Bobbie was immediately ordered to mount guard before the front door,
and Jacky before the kitchen door. She begged
me to speak in a low, whispering voice, so that my
intimate and delicate professional questions should
not be overheard by the monster. Suddenly she
would sit up in bed, and dramatically point to the
evil eye peering at her through a crack in the ceiling.

If I expressed the slightest doubt about his
being there, she would get very angry and excited.
If I affected to share her belief, she would become
very communicative and give me some details of
his history.

This devil of a man, she told me, was a little
undersized ugly Scotchman with a red beard,
about sixty years of age, and of intemperate
habits. He was engaged on some public works
in Lancashire, and had become friendly with her
husband lodging a few doors away. Shortly after
her husband's death he had proposed to her twice,
meeting on both occasions with a decided refusal.
On the second occasion he was drunk, and made
a terrible scene, using all sorts of threats and
frightening her badly. After this he suddenly
disappeared from the neighbourhood only to
return within a few days down her bedroom
chimney in the middle of the night.

It was to escape from him that she had returned
to her native land. At first she heard and saw
nothing of him and was delighted to think that
she had given him the slip. But alas, on the fifth
evening after the removal, while asleep before
the kitchen fire, she was roused by his hideous

laughter, and met his malignant eye glaring at her through a hole in the kitchen door. After that there was no peace.

However, with the coming of the census enumeration of 1891, arrived the fateful hour when she was enabled to place on record the existence of this fiend, and so to exorcise him.

On the Monday morning when the census form was to be collected, she rose early, polished the kitchen poker carefully, achieved a becoming toilet, and awaited the coming of the enumerator. He was the moorland schoolmaster, and a highly nervous and unusually timid man. Knowing something by repute of the lady's madness, he approached the lonely cottage with some trepidation.

The widow received him with quiet determination, summoned the faithful sentinels to their respective posts, locked, bolted, and barred the kitchen door, placing the key in her pocket, seized the kitchen poker, and pointing first to the table, on which were pen and ink and the open census paper, and then to the fiend at that moment riding astride a side of bacon and cackling most horribly, ordered the now trembling schoolmaster to enter the name of one Peter M'Kenzie, aged sixty-three, of Glasgow, as a temporary occupant of Toldrun Cottage. For a moment the pedagogue hesitated, but seeing the poker raised in a threatening attitude, hastily obeyed. Mrs Buckton carefully examined the document, and after being perfectly satisfied that all was in order released the schoolmaster, who was only too glad to escape from such a dreadful ordeal.

From that hour Mr M'Kenzie's attentions

began to wane, his laugh grew less hideous and his eye less malignant, and in a short time ceased from troubling.

She became quite a sane and a rational woman again. When, in after years, I once ventured to refer to him, she only smiled; a far-away dreamy look came into her eyes, and she began to talk again about her pigs and poultry.

George Wilson, as I will call him, was a sheep farmer, nearly sixty years of age, and a widower. Both his sons had left him and gone out into the world. When clothed and in his right mind he was good to look at, with his golden yellow beard now tinged with grey, his deep blue eyes, and imposing stature. His manner was quiet and one of no little charm; he was educated above his station, and was a most agreeable and interesting man to talk to.

The farm was his own property, and he did all the work as far as possible single-handed. The house itself was most picturesquely situated on high ground amid a grove of fir-trees, and was conspicuous for many miles round. I have been able, on a clear day, to see from it a sugar-loaf hill at least thirty-five miles away. It was the last house before the interminable moor began.

His housekeeper was the only other occupant of the comfortable farmhouse.

Owing to some secret worry he began to drink deeply, steadily, and secretly. From some idiosyncrasy the demon very quickly got the upper hand. The man was soon transformed into a dangerous madman. It was extraordinary to those of us who knew him how great and rapid this transformation was.

His faithful housekeeper, who had tried all her powers of persuasion to rescue him from the mad craze but in vain, was at length so terrified by his threats that she was compelled to leave him abruptly.

The sons, who had been summoned, were powerless to interfere, and were ordered off by the mad father.

Slowly and surely he became the terror of his neighbours and the countryside. He threatened all and sundry who opposed his will. He poached indiscriminately, in defiance of all game laws and gamekeepers, but his poaching was only on a small scale and purely to supply his own larder.

In his excursions abroad he always went on horseback with his loaded shot gun under his arm. He was an excellent rider and had a very good horse, so that he seemed to be here, there, and everywhere in no time. He would fire off his gun promiscuously to enforce his threats and terrify his victims, and as he was an excellent shot, no one happily was ever injured, though there were some hairbreadth escapes. It was his custom to descend on lonely farmhouses demanding, or seizing, food and liquor, always with a watchful eye ready to mount his gallant steed and ride away across country.

One morning about eleven o'clock, after tying his horse up in the yard, he invaded my house. Uninvited and with loaded gun he walked into the surgery and began messing about with the drugs and bottles.

My wife very pluckily begged him to come out, but he refused, saying he was a fully qualified doctor, and knew quite well what he was about. However, she managed to entice him into the kitchen, where a hurriedly prepared but substantial meal was temptingly spread out. As he was voraciously hungry, he speedily reached to and made a terrific meal. At its conclusion he asked for a cigar, mounted his horse and rode quietly away.

On another occasion he marched into the village church in the middle of divine worship with his hat on and his shoulders covered with a big flowing red shawl. With some sense of the order of things, he had left the loaded gun at the church door. He took a prominent place in the congregation, interrupted the service with loud amens and extraordinary gestures with his arms. No one was brave enough to tackle him. After his half hour's strange devotions he quietly withdrew, to the great relief of the startled worshippers. I have no doubt many silent prayers of thanksgiving were uttered.

One dark night on a lonely moorland road he gave me quite a bad fright by firing his gun from the hedge bottom behind me. I never saw him because it was too dark, but I knew only too well whose playful trick it was.

Birds of a feather flock together, and many stories of drunken orgies at the lonely farmhouse were reported. Peaceful passers-by were compelled to enter for carouse.

It is incredible on recalling these events that his reign of terror should have lasted so long as nearly three years. His neighbours either were too timid to lay a complaint against him to the authorities, or were reluctant to do so, remembering him as the good and kindly neighbour of bygone years. The clannish feeling is strong, and nearly all of us had a sneaking regard for the man. Of course reports of his misdoings reached the police. The village policeman with a big family, and early prospect of a well-earned pension, was anxious to keep a whole skin. As an old soldier he was a master of strategy and an adept at taking cover. He made a great show of doing things, but it was all masterly inactivity; nothing was accomplished.

From his lofty stronghold, surveying with his hawk-like eye all the kingdoms of the earth, Wilson kept a watchful look-out. When danger threatened and the policeman did pay a perfunctory visit, he retired within, locking and bolting the doors, and sat waiting with loaded gun for developments which never came.

He was no coward, and I am perfectly certain he would have shot at sight anyone who attempted to arrest him on his own premises.

On several occasions in his periodic flying visits to the other dales or lowlands he was arrested and punished for firing off his gun to the public danger, but in his own immediate native land he always escaped scot-free.

It is interesting to note in his case how soon alcoholic insanity will pass away when its cause is withdrawn. On one of his excursions to the lowlands he was arrested and confined in a police-station on the charge of being a dangerous lunatic at large. There was some unavoidable but considerable delay in certifying him, and when the doctors at length arrived for the purpose, he was perfectly quiet, rational, and sane.

The local police authorities having failed to bring him to task, I was one day, after one of his mad pranks, requested to examine him and, if possible, certify him. I saw that my will was in order, and bade my wife an affectionate good-bye. I scarcely believed he would harm me because we had always been excellent friends, but I was invading the precincts of his castle and knew that accidents might happen. I thought it was wiser to go alone, and approached the farm by a circuitous footpath. To my no small relief I found the house deserted. I heard afterwards that he had departed on one of his flying visits up the dale to back of beyond.

However, shortly after this his mad career came to an end. He solved all our difficulties himself, poor fellow, and his own at the same time.

The village idiot was acting as temporary postman one morning, and in passing the open door of the barn of the farm, happened to look in. He saw Wilson suspended by a rope, strangling himself and still in his death struggle. Instead of cutting him down, in his terror he ran away at top speed, and never stopped till he met a passer-by two miles off to whom he reported the occurrence; then of course it was too late to do anything.

The opinion of the countryside was that the idiot was not so daft after all, and that by removing himself quickly from the scene, he had acted with great wisdom and judgment.

It was evidently a very sudden impulse that

prompted Wilson to solve the great problem, because the kettle was found to be boiling, the bacon in slices and the egg ready for the breakfast he never ate.

The last story I will inflict on the reader while on this subject, is one of those events which stir a countryside, are more than a nine days' wonder, and are retold over and over again for years by the peat fireside.

It was also one of great interest to me from a psychological point of view.

There lived in the moorland village a stone-mason then thirty-eight years of age. He came of a well-balanced moorland stock, though I believe eventually two brothers became hard drinkers. He was clever at his job, always in demand, and very industrious. Very rarely he had fits of moodiness and sulkiness.

But he had what was to him a very great grievance. It was the humble station in life to which he had been called. He was appalled at the terrific gap yawning between the poor and the very rich. He hated all rich people and, unlike most Englishmen, specially lords and their ladies. It was really at the bottom a case of pure envy. He broke the tenth commandment many times a day. This grievance became an obsession, and ultimately a delusion.

He was purely a moorland product, but he was the material out of which anarchists are fashioned —one of those poisonous weeds which grow in all lands, even, as it appeared, on moorlands.

He was an intense Radical, but took no interest in politics nor in any particular scheme for the abolition of rich lords. Although a good workman, he had no desire to work very hard and so become richer, nor did he feel inclined to help himself to the good things he coveted. I have no doubt if there had been a society in the village to annihilate lords, he would have cheerfully joined and done his share of the good work.

I know there are weak-minded people who take a sudden fancy to possess the moon, and when they find they cannot get it go raving mad. But it seemed impossible to me that envy alone would drive a man mad.

He was intelligent enough on all other matters, and I had long talks and arguments with him to try and reason him out of his obsession. It was all to no purpose, "Why can't I be a lord and ride in a carriage and pair? Why can't I go fox-hunting? Why can't I dress up like a toff and go to London?" These were samples of his grievance. To him, apparently, there was no satisfactory answer to these questions.

One day when work was rather slack, he got a job at some alterations in the stables of a very rich peer of the realm. If he had been consistent, he should have refused any favour at the hands of such an odious being.

Perhaps it was a case of real personal curiosity to see what actually did occur in the establishment of a real live lord. Evidently the galaxy of foot-men, grooms, gamekeepers, gardeners, horses, and so forth which he saw completely knocked him off his balance. For some days he was very quiet though harping more than usual on his eternal grievance; then one dark winter's morning, after bringing to his wife's bedside the cup of tea he never forgot, he set off on his five-mile walk across country to his work. He never returned home, nor was ever seen alive again. At first his wife felt no uneasiness, thinking that he had got convenient lodgings near his work; but further inquiry elicited the fact that he had never returned to work, nor had anybody heard or seen anything of him.

Search was made up and down dale, but no trace of him could be found. Christmas passed, springtime came, and the poor distracted wife, now at the end of resources, was compelled to apply for parish relief, and to remove to another village in order to obtain employment.

One glorious summer's evening, with a golden sunset lighting the western sky, I was returning homewards along the moorland road with fishing rod over my shoulders, and well-filled creel, thinking what a glorious world it is, when I met a woman hurrying toward me. "The've fun 'im," she said. "Whom?" I asked. "Bob Waddington," she replied, "and I'm off to tell Mary"—his wife.

And this was the strange finding. Within only four hundred yards of Waddington's cottage, adjoining a much frequented footpath, was a small cowshed. In the very diminutive loft, scarcely bigger than a dog kennel, access to which could only be obtained by climbing up the hay-rack, were stored the farmer's hay-forks and hay-rakes. When collecting these, the farmer's son found Waddington strangled by a rope. Being a big man he had done it with his knees on the ground. What a determined suicide!

I went on my way again, wondering sadly that such strange tragedies should happen in such a beautiful world.

That cowshed is still avoided, or passed tremblingly by, from fear of seeing Bob Waddington's ghost.

CHAPTER XI

YORKSHIRE hospitality, like that famous product of the county, the Yorkshire ham, is known the whole world over.

There is no pompous affectation or formality about it, such as one encounters in some lands. But one is always sure of a kindly welcome and that is the true test of hospitality. I have had hundreds of meals in the homes of my patients, from the peer to the pauper, and never failed of this kindly welcome. With the poor this hospitality is an instinctive duty, and with the rich it is a luxury. Yorkshiremen are notoriously the keenest of business men and drive the hardest of bargains, but their hospitality is a thing quite apart.

I have heard it said that Yorkshire men feed you and then rob you, but no statement could be more misleading.

In primitive times the weakest went to the wall. In the struggle for existence those who were unable to fight or defend themselves in face of greater strength or determination, naturally starved. But as civilisation came and spread, there grew correspondingly the obligation to care for the weak, the needy, and the sick. Hospitality, at first a duty, became a virtue, and then more or less an instinct. Tradition says that Guaire, King of Connaught, in the seventh century gave so much in gifts of hospitality that his right arm grew longer than his left.

In the Middle Ages nunneries and monasteries established guest-houses, and dispensed charity to the needy. These have been replaced for better or for worse by the workhouse, the infirmary, and countless charitable institutions. Hospitality had naturally a disarming and elevating effect on those who were entertained, and hence in time came the feeling, that having eaten the bread and salt of another, one must do him no wrong nor speak any evil of him. Instances have been recorded where the chance eating of an enemy's bread and salt has meant the end of a feud.

In mountainous and hilly countries, which were thinly populated, and where the conditions of life were extremely hard and difficult, the obligations of hospitality would be all the more necessary and frequent. We are told that in classical times the inhabitants of the backward and mountainous kingdom of Thessaly enjoyed quite a reputation for generous hospitality. It is therefore quite easy to understand that on the hills and moors of Yorkshire the virtue reaches its acme. There, though the stranger is invariably the object of a natural suspicion, he is, as a guest, assured of a scrupulous hospitality. Even in houses where the word hospitality would not be understood, the thing exists, and the guest is invariably served first. "Come thi ways, sit thee sen down and reach to," is the formula of welcome, and the happiest response is to "reach to with a long arm" and do fullest justice to the well-laid table.

It must not be forgotten that the lives of these people are very lonely ones, and that in that wonderful air, specially after the hard work of sheep-tending, they have huge appetites, and the advent of the stranger is a good and sound excuse to let themselves go. *Hospitis adventus causa bibendi.*

I had an amusing experience once when on foot in a remote district where I was not known. It was a hot scorching day, and I was correspondingly thirsty. I called at a farmhouse for a glass of water. To my surprise my humble request was angrily refused. Does not Hitopadesa say that some straw, a room, water, and in the fourth place gentle words are things never to be refused in good men's houses? I did not even get gentle words. Just as I was turning away I was still further mystified by an offer of milk or beer. Then came the explanation. Pure drinking-water was very precious, because in droughty weather it had to be fetched from quite a long distance.

The only objection I had to the delightful and bountiful hospitality of my friends, was that they insisted on my eating and drinking more than I wanted or was good for me. It was often a very real and a frequently recurring problem how to avoid it without hurting their feelings. At feast and fair the farmers kept open house. Christmas time was a terrible trial, and I was compelled for weeks to run the gauntlet of countless rich plum cakes, fat cheeses, and much good cheer. It was an embarrassment that might easily have been fatal.

I once literally ran away to escape the relentless Yorkshire hospitality. It was in this wise. I had been watching over the safe hatching out of another moorland chick. At these happy events it is the custom to provide hospitality for the refreshment of all who have been assisting at the function, no matter what the hour may be. Substantial feasts at unearthly hours are decidedly provocative of sleeplessness and nightmares. I said good-night to the mother and nurse and descended to the house kitchen to find it momentarily deserted. There were all the good things spread out, but no one to bid me sit down and "reach to." Here at any rate for once was a rare chance to escape. As I happened to be afoot I slipped out quickly, and got about two hundred yards away from the house when I heard the farmer calling loudly for me through the night. Then he began to hurry after me in pursuit, first walking and then running faster and faster. I got on to the moor road, and took the precaution to run on the grass at the side. Sounds carry far on the moorland at night. He kept up the chase for about a mile before he gave it up. Next day he remarked, "What a walker ye be, Doctor, how ye can leg it." They were dreadfully put out at what they thought was their flagrant breach of good manners. It seemed a ridiculous occurrence for a doctor to be running away at top speed with a black bag at three o'clock in the morning, to escape from fried Yorkshire ham, but so it happened.

A patient once consulted me shortly before Christmas for some rather serious dyspeptic trouble. While I was detailing a long list of forbidden foods, I noticed that his face grew longer and longer. At last he burst forth, " Eh, bairn, I wish I had put off till after Kersmass seeing thee."

The degree of hospitality varies according to the means and temperament of the hosts. The predominant factor is the housewife, who sees watchfully to the wants of everybody, and is the last person served. All the household, including servants, "meat" together in the "hoose" or kitchen. Farmhouses are known far and wide as good or bad meat-houses, as the case may be, and in the former the servant question never becomes acute. Even the meanest and most miserly housewife realises the duty of hospitality, and will set her best before you ungrudgingly. Any offer of payment is indeed regarded as an insult.

I have noticed over and over again among these thrifty but hospitable people, that in cases of sickness or undeserved poverty among their neighbours, though they were often generous to a fault in the giving of food or delicacies, they would never under any circumstances part with the smallest coin of the realm.

I shall not easily forget my first professional visit to a Yorkshire dale. Being a Yorkshireman I knew quite well that unless I wished to earn a reputation of being "'igh, 'aughty, and pompey," I must accept on a first visit any hospitality offered me. At the first farmhouse after my consultation was over, I was asked by the farmer, "What will ye tak?" Thinking a little whisky would be the least injurious under the circumstances, I asked for it. The housewife's face became at once solemn and serious and as long as a fiddle before she said, "Ye are welcome reight eneagh to t'drop o' whisky, but we deean't want any mair drunken doctors in t'shop." What a stupid blunder on my part. Then I went on to the next farmhouse where I was also asked what I would "tak." "A glass of milk," I replied, with great self-confidence. But the second housewife's face became, if possible, even more serious and solemn than the previous one's. "Ye are welcome," she explained, "to t'drop o' milk, but we deean't want any mair drunken doctors. Dr Macpherson, when he fust came, used to axe for milk like ye, and thens he axed for whisky which war his ruin." I had escaped from Scylla to Charybdis, and it was all very perplexing. I was informed afterwards that the majority of my predecessors had been topers and "drunken dogs."

Is there any wonder that many country doctors degenerate into drunken doctors in a county like Yorkshire? For many hours of a long night, miles away from home in the depths of winter, one may be tied up at a farmhouse waiting patiently for the hatching of a moor chick. Peat fires give out a delightful smell but not much heat, and it is not always easy to keep warm by them. The father, full of the traditional hospitality, possibly begins "wetting the baby's head" hours before its arrival, and is soon jovial and convivial. If there is a little anxiety, all the more reason to combat it. He of course presses and expects you to join him,

and it requires some strength of will to refuse.
For my own reputation's sake I made it a firm
rule never to touch a drop of alcohol till the babe
was safely in the world. On the long, bitterly
cold drives in winter, I was often kindly invited
to have "summat warming."

The teetotalers may protest as much as they
like, but there is no pick-me-up so effective as a
whisky and soda when one is thoroughly jaded
after a hard day's work and too tired to eat.
Worries vanish as if by magic and appetite returns.
I have tried both the teetotal and the other plan.
A farmer once explained to me that his infallible
remedy for agricultural depression was a "sup o'
gin and watter," and that the outlook was always
brighter afterwards—*Ebrietas sollicitis animis onus
eximit.*

A thrifty but generous Yorkshireman once
scored very cleverly off me, and chuckled heartily
over his success. I attended him occasionally for
attacks of syncope after hunting. On one occasion
after being summoned hurriedly to his bedside, he
asked if I was perfectly sure the attack was exactly
similar to the previous ones. Having replied in
the affirmative, he said with a most triumphant
expression on his face, "Then you need not send
me any more medicine at present, because I have
three-quarters of the last bottle you made in the
wine-cellar in a cool place." I don't know to this
day how many vintages of old physic he had, but
I do know there was some very excellent old port
which I helped him occasionally to drink.

I arrived at one confinement hours before time
to find the anxious father had been wetting the

baby's head in a thorough business-like and anticipatory fashion. To escape his hospitable attention I said I would lie down in the spare bedroom.

Ten minutes afterwards he opened the bedroom door, remarking, "This ligging (lying) down is a varra good idea, Doctor, an' I'll come and keep ye company an' lig wi' ye," and immediately lay down beside me, a friendly enough proceeding but very objectionable. I made an excuse at once to get rid of him, by suggesting something for the patient's good, and then bolted the door. He returned shortly afterwards, and after persistent requests for admission which I silently ignored, presently sat down on the bedroom door-mat, with his back to the door, and slept soundly for three hours afterwards.

It was the custom of the country that the birth of the baby should be celebrated by eating a big fat plum cake called the baby-cake, made by the expectant mother, who would relate proudly how much good butter and how many eggs she had used. It was afterwards consumed by callers who came to see the mother and new arrival ; and on these occasions in the "Bettermy" farmhouses port or good home-made wine was produced. The baby-cake takes the place of the christening cake in other places, and the doctor is invariably requested to cut the first piece. My wish on these occasions was always "That the boy or girl might grow up to be the father or mother of a very large family and so help to keep the doctors out of the workhouse," and always received as quite a good joke.

Most excellent home-made wines were made by the clever housewives. These were blackberry, gooseberry, cowslip, rhubarb, colt's-foot, elderberry, and beetroot. Some had been kept for some years and were decidedly potent and very clear. A beverage frequently brewed too on those moorlands was a species of mead called botchet, made from the moorland honey. It was much too sweet to be pleasant taking, and decidedly heady. "Leggy" the natives called it because of its effects on the gait. Many bees were kept in the district. The moorland honey has a flavour peculiarly its own, and I thought it much more delicious than the ordinary variety. It is perhaps a trifle bitter, and not agreeable to everybody's taste.

In the many moorland inns it was possible to get a good glass of local ale, and the gin was also always good and reliable, generally Nicholson's product, but of the nondescript fiery stuff which they invariably gave you whether you asked for Irish, Scotch whisky, or brandy, the least said the better.

A retired farmer I knew many years ago and whose funeral I describe elsewhere in detail possessed a superlative reputation for lavish hospitality and excellent liquor. Of the latter Krofer Duffield had never been known to run short. Once, however, a consecutive nightly and crowded carouse, together with roads blocked with snow, which prevented any replenishment, brought his supply perilously near vanishing point, and his reputation was in danger. He might possibly in emergency have borrowed, but such an humiliation had never arisen. When some old "particulars" turned up for the third night in succession, he asked anxiously, "Are ye lads making a night on it?"   "Nay! nay!" they replied, "we gan early." Reassured on this point he produced the good gin. But on these tiresome forgetful fellows sat, filling their glasses high, "cracking away" and "capping" each other's yarns, till the precious liquor had nearly gone.

Asking to be excused, the host hastily filled a two-gallon stone jar with water, corked and sealed it.   Then he turned it on its side, kicking it into his parlour.   Retiring again to fill a white top hat, of which he was inordinately proud during its summer wear, with a pound of tobacco, he returned to bang it down on the parlour table.   After locking the room door, and putting the key in his pocket, he gave out, "Now ye lads, noan on us quit this room till we've supped all t'gin an' smeeaked all t'baccy."

All these merry fellows could carry their liquor well, but this challenge alarmed them.   They emptied their glasses and departed, while Krofer Duffield more than added to a hospitable pre-eminence, which is immortal on the moorlands.

There is a story told locally of a visitor to a ducal house in the dales for the winter's hunting. He was an impecunious, sponging, south-country colonel who, having ruined himself with riotous living, was now anxious to help others at the same game.   He was known as a very hard drinker, with great carrying capacity.   One day while discussing the great shire with his host, he remarked, "I have always heard that Yorkshiremen were men of unbounded stomach and able to carry their whack of wine well, but they are a poor lot

that I have met so far at your table, Duke."
"Egad, no, Colonel," replied the duke, "there are
scores of good Yorkshiremen who can easily see
you under the table." "Well, Duke, I should
like to meet them, that's all." There was a
suggestive challenge about this final remark, which
the duke, for the reputation of the county, could
not very well ignore. He recognised that the
colonel was a very hard nut to crack, and that
the matter required very careful handling. His
house steward, with whom he talked the matter
over, at once suggested, "Why not ask Jack Myers
for once, Your Grace?" Jack Myers was a tenant
farmer on the ducal estate, who had the notoriety
of carrying his liquor better than any man in the
district. His admirers and friends asserted that
it was an utter impossibility to make him drunk.
He was a good-looking fellow too, of fine physique,
with decent manners, and an abundant gift of
native wit. "The very man," said the duke, and
immediately sent the steward with a personal
invitation, explaining the plot, and at the same
time offering the gift of a new suit of clothes
quite *à la mode*. Myers accepted with unconcealed
delight, saying that it was just his "game to a
hay seed."

On the fateful night the duke, in high good
humour, beamed on his well-filled table, confident
that the repute of the shire of many acres was in
safe hands. Myers, perhaps the handsomest and
best set-up man in the room, was at first shy and
reserved, but when the wine commenced to flow
freely, his natural wit came to his help. One by
one these gallant sportsmen went under the table

and were carried to bed. The duke's turn came in time, and then only the fittest remained. The colonel, slightly truculent and quarrelsome, sat far into the night *vis-à-vis* the good-humoured Yorkshireman. Many great episodes of hunting and racing were recalled. Then the colonel began to balance his words, shooting out his sentences, a certain sign that the helpless stage of inco-ordination was near. The supply of good wine had temporarily run out. "Ring the bell," jerked the colonel, "we want some more wine." "Ring it yourself," said Myers. "It's just behind you, I'm not your servant." The colonel looked anxiously round, fixing in his eye the bell's position, and after glaring angrily at the Yorkshireman for some minutes, pulled himself together with one supreme concentrated effort. He got up and managed to walk to the bell, but unfortunately in returning one foot caught in a skin rug, and down he went. He was a big man and fell very heavily. The end had come suddenly, and there he lay helplessly and hopelessly drunk. When the footmen answered the summons Myers said quietly to these astonished menials, "Take that fellow to bed, he's as drunk as a fiddler, and bring another bottle of wine." The colonel was carried to bed, and another bottle of wine brought in. After drinking this with leisurely deliberation, Myers asked for his horse, walked steadily to the great doors of the castle, mounted, and rode into the night.

The colonel was unmercifully chaffed. So pleased was the duke that he invited Myers to dinner again and, it was said, even remitted him half a year's rent.

A small manufacturer on the hills, although hardworking and industrious, used such bad judgment in buying that he continually found himself in financial stress. He had, too, an enormous appetite and was a notorious trencherman. On the third occasion when his creditors had been called together, he was awaiting in an adjoining room with a great friend for their decision whether he should be made a bankrupt or not. The pangs of hunger assailed him because it was now long past his usual hour of dining. Suddenly his friend saw him stop his restless pacing and begin tapping his stomach. Then he heard him address it thus, "Noo thens, thee be quiet, thou's awlus had twenty shillings to t'pund, whatever t'others have had."

The local preachers were always most hospitably entertained, and thoroughly the majority seemed to anticipate and enjoy it. Some of them ate so much that one got the impression they had eaten nothing during the previous week.

One terrific guzzler over-ate his welcome so much that he was occasionally allowed to fall back on his own humble parcel of refreshment. However he discovered a very ingenious and effective way of turning the tables on his village hosts. At the commencement of the service he hung his red handkerchief holding his food in a conspicuous position near the pulpit, and at intervals in the course of the sermon contrived to draw attention to it. After making some statement he would say, "It is as true as that thear handkerchief holds my bit of food." Overcome with remorse, quite a deputation of hosts waited for him at the chapel door, pressing their hospitality. After listening to all the invitations in turn, he replied with great condescension, "I will go with Mr Hogg"—naming the host who kept the best "meat house."

The product of the county in greatest repute is the Yorkshire home-fed ham. It is really world famous. When travelling abroad I have often been assured that the ham I was consuming was "Vrai jambon d'York," though it had scarcely the faintest resemblance to the genuine article. There could not have been a more captious critic. In addition to the skill and care in curing, time is a very great factor in its creation. It must be ripe and mellow and not too lean.

Boiled or baked ham is the joint of honour and chief "belly timber" on all occasions of Yorkshire hospitality, at agricultural shows, feasts, fairs, funerals, harvest homes, and chapel functions. Well-baked ham is much superior to boiled ham. And to-day the smell of fried ham at once brings back the memory of happy days spent on the moorlands, of the hospitality of those kindly people, and the many great friendships I made.

Once when he was "market fresh," one of my patients insisted that I should have some gin, which I declined. "I'll mak ye tak it," he said. As he was a big, powerful man and very quarrelsome, there might have been trouble, but his daughter behind his back made signs urging me to take it, and for peace sake I gave way.

Only the previous week when market fresh he had called on his son-in-law at a neighbouring farm, with whom he was in temporary disagreement. In order to lay violent hands on him to enforce an argument he proceeded to chase him round a fourteen-acre field, but handicapped by weight and liquor came in a very bad second. These proceedings were witnessed by some neighbours returning from the local market on the high road, who to this day refer to it as the great "Milne Rigg Race." The man nearly died after his strenuous effort.

The glories of Yorkshire ham must not lead me to forget those of that twin pillar of Yorkshire fame—Yorkshire pudding.

A Yorkshire farmer, staying at an old-fashioned London hotel, when asked by the waiter if he liked Yorkshire pudding, astonished the diners by replying, "Loike Yorkshire pudden, I sud think I deea, bless ye I've eeaten yakkers (acres) of it i' my toime."

CHAPTER XII

THREEAPINS AN' DIFFERINS

I REGRET to say my moorland friends were very
obstinate, very quarrelsome, and very irreconcilable
in their quarrels. Hill men from earliest times in
all countries have been more quarrelsome and
pugnacious than their lowland brothers. They
are more remote from the influence of civilisation,
are stronger and hardier, and more primitive in
their instincts.

In former days a little judicious shedding of
blood relieved the tension, and bitter enemies
thereby often became excellent friends; but the
good old game of fighting has long passed away
from the Yorkshire highlands.

To-day there is only the quarrelling left, which
is in consequence all the more bitter and relentless. My friends quarrelled in deadly earnest; they
never forgave and they never forgot. Sometimes
the feud went on from father to son. They
quarrelled over their grazing and sporting rights,
over their sheep and stock, over trickery in
bargaining, and of course over those old bones
of contention—wills, religion, and money. The
majority of them called themselves Radicals, and
terribly bitter politicians many of them were.

A Westmoreland friend of mine, in practice for

many years in a mountainous district, quite early noticed this proneness to quarrel among his fell-side patients, and tried to account for it by various theories. The conclusion he came to was that the causation was climatic; he thought their livers were sluggish from constant exposure to the cold winds so long prevalent during the year, which rendered them peevish and irritable. That might have something to do with it of course. The destiny of nations has been changed before to-day by an attack of indigestion.

But it is only too true that my moorland friends were for ever "threeaping and differing."

The inhabitants of one moorland village were, however, an extraordinarily marked contrast to their neighbours. They never seemed to quarrel, were always amiable and good-tempered, gave one a friendly salutation and greeting, and in sickness could not do enough for one another.

I one day made the remark to the Squire of this village, that of all the twelve or more villages in my practice, the inhabitants of this village were incomparably the best-mannered and most agreeable to attend. My remark evidently pleased him very much, his face fairly beamed, and he nodded most significantly to his wife across the tea-table. Then he told me how this delightful state of affairs had been brought about in his little domain.

The previous Squire, a distant relative from whom he inherited the property, had been a very saintly man, with great force of character and high ideals. His health had always been delicate and prevented him from marrying, but he was exceedingly fond of children, and took the deepest personal interest in the moral and spiritual welfare of all the village children, from their earliest years. He taught them in Sunday school, remembered all their birthdays, called them by their Christian names, took them out long walks in turn, reading to them the great open book of nature, and it must be added did not spare them a very vigorous application of the rod when native sin required it. The good seed fell on fertile ground, and here was the rich harvest, many long years after he and his beloved sister were laid to rest. Those he taught so well and so lovingly were now parents and grandparents, and the lapse of years and experience of life had added to their gentleness and sweet reasonableness.

Though they quarrelled so heartily amongst themselves, my moorland friends instinctively presented a common and hostile front to "foreigners" who ventured to invade their precincts.

I took to task one day a huge hard-bitten, weather-beaten moorland giant, for this unfriendly attitude. "Yans nae good," he retorted, "unless he comes frae ower thaar," pointing to the frowning moors beyond. This was conclusive. These were England to him and his brethren.

"I'se glad to be back i' England again," a patient whom I had sent away, remarked on his return. They thought little of London and all large towns. "What do you think of London?" a Yorkshire Squire inquired of a tenant up for a Royal Show. "I reckon nowt tae it. I can't get a *Darlington* no ways," was his reply. The *Darlington and Stockton Times* is the most widely read paper in North Yorkshire.

Two agricultural friends of mine being pestered by two men selling newspapers, answered them angrily in the broadest Yorkshire, "Git yam, yah ragabush" (get home you rubbish). "Come a-wye Bill," said one to the other. "Deean't ye see, they're them narsty furriners."

When farms fell vacant, and no tenants were available from among the younger sons of the clans, the foreigner came in. If he hailed from other moorlands then he knew the game, walked warily, and in time panned in with the rest. But should he be a luckless lowlander, then he was in for a terrible time of it. Every hand was against him at fairs, at markets, at sales, and in all bargainings. His grazing rights were disregarded and his stock were harried. Stories reflecting on his credit or morality were invented or magnified, and in a thousand little ways he was worried and persecuted. Some gave the game up soon.

I knew one, an excellent fellow and a local preacher, who struggled bravely on for fifteen years before owning himself beaten. He was obliged to take a farm in the adjacent lowlands.

A most remarkable instance occurred in my own village, and if I had not had almost daily evidence I could not have conceived it possible that such persecution could continue through a whole long life. When I first knew this man he was a fine old fellow of seventy. He came of a farming stock, and fifty years before had taken a grazing farm near the village. He was industrious and hard-working. For a time things went badly with him and he became bankrupt, but with great determination and struggling managed to pay his creditors in full. He was a zealous Churchman, and had frequently been nominated vicar's warden. He was a powerfully built man of fine physique, able to take care of himself, and did when occasion arose. He always tried to stand his corner in any movement for the public weal.

All these facts should have been in his favour, and should have appealed to the Yorkshireman's sense of fair play. But not at all. From the day of his coming his neighbours never ceased to use him with envy, hatred, malice, and all uncharitableness. Time had very little influence in softening their attitude. In his old age unfortunately he made a slip. It was nothing immoral, but he gave away some woman who had confided in him. Then came the long-sought opportunity. They were at him like a pack of wolves, and hounded him out of his church-wardenship, and one or two honorary offices he held.

I liked the man, was friendly with him, and employed him and tried hard to account for this life-long animosity. There was certainly a slight flavour of the religious hypocrite about him, but that was all. Far greater hypocrites than he abounded in the land.

Where there was no "stint"[1] of the open pasturage of the moor, there naturally the quarrels and feuds were the fiercest.

Between two clans in particular there had been enmity for over one hundred and fifty years. Violent quarrels and even violence were frequent,

[1] The "stint" of moorland means the apportionment of the sheep to free pasturage in proportion to the size of the freehold.

till one day it was the old story of the way of a
man with a maid.

A son of one married a daughter of the other.
Their first child I brought into the world. All
went well for three years. Then another dreadful
quarrel arose. The father invaded his son-in-law's
house, and carried back his daughter and her baby
by main force. Though happily married she had
the feud in her bones, and was not by any means
unwilling to go back to her old home.

I happened at the time to mention this incident
to a friend who had just returned from a long
fishing holiday in Hungary, and he told me that
an exactly similar incident had occurred in the
district where he had stayed.

No Jew, Greek, or Armenian loves a bargain
better than a Yorkshireman. He reverences the
whole ritual, and goes through the farcical
preliminaries with the utmost seriousness and
solemnity. More value may be spent by the
parties to the bargain and their attendant satellites
in the drinks and refreshment than the amount
perhaps for hours at issue. But when once the
bargain has been struck with the forcible smack of
the hand, it is most scrupulously regarded. It's
a bond more binding than any legal document.
But should any low trickery be brought to light
afterwards then there is war to the knife, and a
bitter life-long quarrel may result.

A parson patient of mine bought a ham from
one of his parishioners who was a very bigoted
Nonconformist. On the Sunday following the purchase this farmer turned up at morning service,
and in the evening all the various members of his

household were at church. But they never came again. Meeting the farmer one day, the parson remarked how pleased he had been to see him and all his family at church, asking him if he had liked the service. "It war all varra nice and coomfortable and it war a good company, bud ye see it war that thear ham ye bowt on me. Ye gave me a turn, so I thowt it only reet to give ye a turn teea." The true spirit of bargaining of course.

Though the moorlanders were jealous enough about their sheep and stock rights, and quarrelled incessantly about them, they never seemed to be jealous of their women folk. There were alien children everywhere, and everybody knew who their fathers were except the children themselves. I was repeatedly asked by the mothers whom these children resembled, and they were evidently very proud to enlighten me. I remember once being asked before a room full of people, by the mother of a farmer's wife, herself the wife of a highly respected farmer, who her daughter was the "spit and image of." I knew of course to whom she was alluding but affected ignorance, and received a sound rating for my dullness. The girl was a squire's daughter.

Sexual jealousy is a most variable trait in human nature, as every doctor well knows. An old medical friend told me of the case of a man who was almost insanely jealous of his wife, and insisted on being present at her confinement. He had approached four doctors in turn who all refused his odd request. My friend effected a compromise. The husband sat throughout his wife's ordeal, with his back to the bed under a kind of awning specially constructed for the occasion. Fortunately Dame Nature was very kind and no complications arose. I was once discussing with a friend, a former fellow-student at a London hospital, then in practice in town, the strange anomalies of human nature. He remarked that in his practice there was an instance of a widow, who had formerly held a good position in decent middle class society, living on the immoral earnings of her three daughters, and wondered that such a thing should be possible. Curiously enough I had shortly before in my own remote moorland village come across an exactly parallel case though in a humbler sphere.

Some of my patients were so contradictious, that all that it was necessary to do in order to get my wishes executed was to suggest the exact opposite.

How stubbornly obstinate some of these people were.

Occasionally when a man had been much moved by some untoward event in his life, he would express himself very assertively about it; and should this assertion, uttered in the presence of witnesses, imply some definite course of action or line of conduct in the future, then it became more than assertion, it had almost the force of an oath, to be strictly observed as a question of personal pride and honour. There must be no softening of the heart as time went on, but rather ever a sterner hardening.

I knew a country joiner and carpenter, who was an industrious, clever, and an honest workman. One day, unfortunately, high words arose between him and the vicar over some work he had done on the church pulpit, and before witnesses he expressed himself very assertively and emphatically about Church parsons. Very shortly afterwards a new vicar was preferred to the living, who was a rich man and desirous of spending a large sum in repairs and alterations to the vicarage. He sent for this excellent man, and together they spent an hour looking over the contemplated work. To the vicar the man appeared very taciturn and almost absent-minded, but in reality a terrible struggle was going on within him between self-advantage and self-pride. The latter at last got the upper hand, and when finally the vicar requested him to commence work at once, he fiercely turned round on him, and hissed out: "—I sed—I'de—never—deea—a-nother—job—fur—a Chetch parson—AN' I'll—warrant ye I weeant—Good arterneean."

George Ashby quarrelled with his life-long friend Robert Kaye over a business transaction, and asserted before witnesses that he would never, as long as he lived, cross his threshold again. As time went on his feelings towards Robert underwent some softening and inwardly, or "bottomly," as they say in Yorkshire, he would have liked to be reconciled, but his strong assertion anent the threshold always stood in the way. However, a resourceful friend of both men suggested a golden bridge. Why not take up the threshold, and afterwards replace it by a new one? He approached both George Ashby and Robert Kaye, and both were more than agreeable to this solution. The threshold was taken up, and George Ashby re-entered his friend's house after thirty years' absence.

Two Yorkshire brothers, William and John

Bickerdike, quarrelled. How the quarrel arose does not concern us, but it was a very real and bitter one, and for forty years, though living in the same village and nearly opposite to one another, they completely ignored each other's existence. They were both men of some substance and position, bore excellent characters, and had many friends. These had made repeated efforts to reconcile the excellent fellows, but without success. They remained implacably hostile, hard as adamant or moorland boulder.

One day John fell ill, took to his bed, and was soon like to die.

The mutual friends were much distressed and, after putting their heads together, decided that one last effort should be made to reconcile these unforgiving brothers.

William was first approached, and after some considerable hesitation, said he "was willin." John likewise hesitated but in the end was also "willin."

So the brothers met and broke the long silence of forty years.

Of course no allusion was made to the quarrel, but they had quite an affecting talk of happy days spent together before it took place, of their old father and mother, and many interesting events; finally, William hoped John would go straight to Heaven, and John in turn hoped he would meet William there when the latter's time came. They shook hands warmly and bade farewell. But before he left the house, William was hastily summoned back to the sick man's bedside. John had something very important to say.

He found John sitting bolt upright in bed,

whereas he had left him laid quite flat. "Now, William," said John very solemnly, and impressively raising his hand, "Now, William, if I get better all this is for nowt."

One Yorkshire lady was a thorn in my side for several years. She was a widow, fairly well educated, comfortably off, and wielded no little influence in the community. She and two or three others had remained faithful in their allegiance to a distant doctor, who at one time had had quite a number of patients in this particular village. She took the defection of the others very much to heart, and made it quite a personal matter. She would follow me in and out of houses with mischievous and meddlesome intent. It was not so much what she said as the way she said it, or what she left unsaid. I often found her waiting in the sickroom for my visit, of course at the patient's invitation. I could have ordered her out, but that would have led to a quarrel with the people, and a country doctor should avoid a quarrel at all costs. It will do him more harm in the end than even professional incapacity.

She would sit through the interview in grim silence, and beyond raising an eyebrow significantly now and again, gave no sign of life. She was really a very astute person, and I regarded her as a formidable if not a bitter enemy.

However, one day her special idol, Dr Johnson, died rather suddenly, and, worse still, she herself was taken ill shortly afterwards, though not dangerously. Then ensued a struggle between loyalty to the dead and her own obstinate self on the one hand, and greater convenience, less expense, and the calling in of an entirely new man with new ways on the other. She made herself much worse worrying over the question before she decided to call in the devil she knew, in preference to the devil she didn't know.

It was a tremendous capitulation, and she made up her mind to make things as disagreeable and unpleasant as possible for me. Nothing I could do for her was right. Each bottle of medicine tried made her worse, my hands blistered her delicate skin when they touched her; I never felt her pulse like Dr Johnson, and to my stethoscope she much objected. Poor Dr Johnson, she explained, used no trumpets and such things, but would put his soft gentle hand on her chest and pronounce, "Mrs Thackeray you have the congestion." Then finally she would shed a few tears, and between her sobs exclaim, "Poor Dr Johnson! Poor Dr Johnson!"

Every day it was the same, till at last my patience was quite worn out. I had had more than enough of poor Dr Johnson and the miserable woman's querulous plaints.

"Yes! Yes!" I joined in, "poor Dr Johnson, but be of good cheer, you shall soon see the dear man again."

She turned very pale, and stared at me in strained surprise for a few minutes.

"What did you say?" she gasped at last.

"That you must cheer up, for you will very soon see the doctor again."

"I don't understand," she said.

"I am making all arrangements for your seeing your dear old friend as soon as possible."

"You surely don't mean you intend to poison me!" she shrieked.

"Yes," I replied, "and I shall do the job thoroughly too."

Then she burst into violent sobbing and genuine tears, and only when exhausted did I talk gently and kindly to her like a Father Confessor.

What a magic transformation was effected. From that hour she was as good as gold, and till she died we were the greatest possible friends.

Another Yorkshire lady, also a widow but of higher degree, with extensive possessions, had in like manner great confidence in Dr Johnson. She was on friendly terms with this genial man and good all-round sportsman, and one day asked his assistance and advice in arranging a shooting party for her. This was gladly given, and gradually the doctor in course of time took entire charge of all her shooting arrangements.

Unfortunately there was a strain of self-conceit in the doctor's character, and in this enviable position he rather lost his head, or in other words could not carry his corn properly; with the result that he and the old lady quarrelled. It won't be a quarrel for long, thought the doctor, because the supply of those precious and special pills he dispensed for her at a guinea a box would soon run out, and the old lady must surely have forgotten how indispensable they were to her in occasional attacks of the colic. But the old lady had not forgotten. She had wisely sent some of them to be analysed, and on learning that they were only composed of ginger was more annoyed than ever with poor Dr Johnson.

One of my predecessors quarrelled with a small Yorkshire squire. I can just recall the latter as a big, tall, fine-looking and imposing man, and a splendid specimen of his class. He and the doctor had been great cronies for many years, and the only subject of discord to disturb this friendship was the shocking state of the squire's *ratione tenuræ* roads, which of course the doctor was obliged to use every day.

"Wait till I persuade them to make me surveyor, then I will make you keep your roads in better order," was the latter's frequent threat uttered half in jest and half in earnest.

In those days surveyors of roads were appointed annually by the different townships, and the usual practice was to choose only those who would spend the least, with the result that the roads were uniformly bad.

Eventually the doctor got his wish, was appointed surveyor, and proceeded at once to carry out his threat. The long friendship was irretrievably broken, the squire swearing that neither the doctor nor his successors should ever attend him or his family again. The squire's descendants have made good his adjuration to this day, much to their own inconvenience.

Eight of the doctor's successors have come and gone, and not one has been called in. I only once ventured to call at this house to report about a tenant who was *in extremis*. I was not allowed to cross the threshold, nor could anyone have been less heartily welcomed.

One day I was called to what was the most

"uncomeatable" farm in the whole district, to see a woman who was reported to be very ill from consumption. She had come unexpectedly from another dale to her grandparents and her old home, in the hope that her native air might effect a cure.

I found her in the last stage of consumption, almost a skeleton, though her face, as is often the case with the consumptive, was still rather plump. I prescribed a "bottle" to relieve her pressing symptoms. On my second visit I had a very warm and friendly welcome from her. She told me my "stuff" had from the first dose gone straight to the spot, putting new life into her, expressed regret that she had not consulted me before, and finally made a number of complimentary remarks about my skill.

I went away feeling quite sorry for her and thinking what a sensible woman she was. But my third visit was a decidedly *mauvais quart d'heure*. She told me she wished she had never set "ees" on me, that my stuff was "nowt" but poisonous "muck" and had nearly finished her off, and called me all the names she could put her tongue to. She had an astounding vocabulary. I was a "nasty good fur nowt," "a daft heeaded barmpot," "a dothery bletherheead," and finally I was "fit fur nowt but pigmeat." Then with collected and concentrated effort she spat full in my face covering me all over with her disgusting saliva.

In no amiable or enviable mood I went on to the moorland vicarage to lunch. Seeing that I had been put out by something, the gentle wife of the vicar asked me what was the matter. I told my story, and instead of sympathising with me over my disgusting treatment they both began to laugh. They then explained their amusement. It appears that this woman had been housemaid with them for some years, and they knew her only too well. Though excellent in every other way, she was exceedingly quarrelsome.

When her mother first took her to the vicarage, she said very decidedly to the vicar's wife, "Noo then, Mrs Jones, this lass o' oors is a reet wurker, varra industrious and varra clean, but she's awlus threeapin, an' gets hersen intiv strange tantrums noos an' thens. But ye mun tak nae noatice. Just up wi' yer fist and hit 'er ower t'nappercracker (head) or onnyways I'se noan sa partickler, bud "— very impressively—"mind ye just fell 'er. That'll larn 'er."

It was difficult to imagine this gentle, gracious lady "felling" a stalwart moorside maid.

In the days when surpliced choirs were becoming the fashion, an offer of the gift of surplices was made by a prominent member of the congregation of a Yorkshire church, and gratefully accepted by the vicar and church-wardens who, together with the bulk of the congregation, were equally anxious for the innovation. The great obstacle, however, was that the most generous and the most influential member of the congregation, a stern unbending Protestant, was bitterly opposed to it. There was every prospect of a deadlock over the matter, when an ingenious compromise and way out of the *impasse* was suggested and agreed to by the vicar and wardens. The great man sat in the north aisle, and his only view of the obnoxious surplices was through a narrow space between the pulpit and the pillar of the chancel arch. A board was fixed to fill it and remained there till in the course of time he became reconciled to the eyesore.

The following story illustrates the extreme reluctance of the Yorkshireman to own up when he knows he is quite in the wrong.

Two ladies driving alone over the moor met a man with a horse and cart, and had great difficulty in passing him on the narrow road. He became exceedingly rude and abusive, so much so that the ladies afterwards wrote a strongly worded letter of complaint to his employer, whose name they had recognised on the cart. The latter wrote most courteously in reply, promising that the man would come to apologise. When the carter arrived, he was shown into the ladies' presence and at once remarked, "Ah think ye be the two laadies Ah toad to gan to Hell t'uther daay." "Yes, we were," they replied. "Well, ye've nae 'casion," was the very curt apology.

If individuals could be so very quarrelsome and obstinate, it followed of course that communities could be equally so.

One day when the countryside was attending the weekly market of the little country town of Muxley, a terrible snowstorm and blizzard occurred, and in an incredibly short time the roads were hopelessly blocked, and the walls and hedges obliterated by huge snowdrifts.

It was really a record storm, as I remember to my own cost and discomfort.

News reached a large moorland village that its

market people had stuck fast on the moorland high road, and that all their conveyances were more or less completely buried.

A large rescue party was hastily formed and set off on its mission of salvation, with the village blacksmith at its head. The very first man they found was the village parson, who with his pony and cart was almost out of sight in a deep ditch. It happened at the time that this parson was in very bad odour with the parishioners. There had been much “threeapin” and “differin,” and the parson was for the moment the most unpopular man in the village.

Moorland wit and gumption was not slow to recognise that here was a golden opportunity sent by the gods to more than square the long account. There was a hurried consultation, after which the village blacksmith delivered the ultimatum of the party.

“Noo bide theesen wi’ patience and lang sufferin’, fur thou’s t’varra last man we sall dig out. Thar’s lang Tom, Bill of Sturrocks, and Toldrum, Stubbings, Tommie wid t’lads, and Tommie wid t’lasses an a seet mair as are all wanted at heeam to milk t’coos, feed t’pigs, sarve t’calves, and tend t’sheep. Thar’s Cobbler Jack has got sum mair leather, an thar’s Mary Harper with a seet o’ groceries which ’ll be ez wet ez mook. Noo we deeant want thee till Sunday, so bide thaar till we’ve laated all t’rest.”

So the poor parson instead of being the first was the very last man to be rescued.

CHAPTER XIII

DE SENECTUTE

CENTENARIANS and very old people are always objects of great personal interest, specially in the country, where they stand out on the horizon of life as human landmarks, living monuments of past years and events, and links between present and past generations. We are all proud of any family longevity, and love to recall the doings and sayings of our wondrously old relations. Until we ourselves suddenly realise that we are old, we live on hope and our hope is to live long days and not grow old. We envy these old patriarchs and strive to emulate them. But old age is not always enviable. The cheery optimistic Nestor is a treasure all too rare. Too often the days of old age are, as the psalmist reminds us, days of strength turned to labour and sorrow, full of discomfort, illusion, prejudice, and strange paradoxes of wisdom and childishness.

Old people, too, are often crabby and disagreeable, and for ever asserting their prerogative of experience. The ancient hypocrite who, having sown wild oats, makes a parade of enforced virtues, is the most intolerable of beings.

Some have a lonely old age and are left stranded on the sands of time.

One such among my patients possessed a surpassing vitality, his memory was marvellous, and his eyes fairly used to blaze in their sunken orbits. He was ninety-eight. He had outlived all his children and grandchildren, and only one great-granddaughter was left. His own stock had all died out, and there he was, a grim, pathetic, solitary figure, anxiously waiting for the Silent Messenger who seemed to have forgotten him or passed him by.

Another one, by contrast, whom I knew, was anxiously cared for by his surrounding descendants. He enjoyed excellent health and the good things of life to the very end. He had been a good all-round sportsman, and was an excellent bridge player. His last message to his friends on his death-bed was, "Tell them I am going No Trumps, and hope to get a Grand Slam."

It is interesting to note how our feelings about our own age vary as life goes on. In childhood and early manhood we like to be thought older than our years. When we attain our prime of manhood we proclaim it and glory in it. Then as years roll on we begin to conceal our age, till one day we suddenly discover that we have achieved old age and are then intensely proud of it.

A woman of course is as old as she looks, till the day dawns when even she cannot resist the temptation to announce a distinguished old age.

One lady whom I knew, a member of an old county family, never gave herself away till her hundredth birthday, when she wrote to her friends announcing the fact.

In my extensive moorland practice there were

quite a number of Methuselahs. Hereditary influence and a healthy environment of course played their part in their production, but it was really and truly a case of survival of the fittest.

Local government inquiries into water and drainage schemes having obliged me to go into vital statistics and figures, I was astonished to find that the average death rate, spread over a number of years, was not much lower than that of the towns. Recurring epidemics of infectious diseases increased it. Deaths were more frequent in early life and up to the forties, but beyond that they dropped considerably.

In one year in a large parish I had five deaths, two under two years, the others at ninety-seven, ninety, and eighty-six years. In one moorland parish of about forty farms there were no deaths for two years nor any burial in the churchyard.

Man cannot add a cubit to his stature, but he can add to his years. Some of these ancient folk were not as old as they pretended to be.

One vain-glorious gaffer suddenly tacked on ten years. I was attending him in his last illness and asked his correct age. "Eighty-eight," he replied very promptly. But I pointed out to him that a year before when I was attending him he had given his age as seventy-seven.

However, he stuck to his eighty-eight, and his wife who, as I found out afterwards, was the instigator of this addition, backed him up and made herself very disagreeable about my doubts.

On the coffin-lid a few days afterwards were the figures eighty-eight. His real age was of course seventy-eight, and the true reason, I discovered afterwards, of the addition, was the desire not to fall too far behind an elder brother who had died at ninety-two.

I was once intensely interested in hearing some evidence in a celebrated right-of-way case. Of course a great number of ancient witnesses to the truth were called on both sides.

Among them was one who said his age was ninety, but he was not quite sure about it. He gave his evidence very well and convincingly, but the examining Counsel, after rapid calculation of the years covered by the various periods mentioned, pointed out to him that by his own statements his real age must be one hundred and thirty instead of ninety years. "Yes," he replied proudly, "I knew I was terrible old."

What a wonderful phalanx of "old aged men" used to present themselves at these government inquiries, to oppose, by their impressive presence and their evidence, what was in their eyes a useless waste of public money.

Although many of these active and sturdy survivals of the fittest called themselves Liberals or Radicals, they were the Toriest of Tories in their fierce opposition to any new-fangled ideas of efficient drainage, pure water, or in fact any innovation proposed for the good of the community. They deemed themselves to be in their own persons so many irrefutable arguments against any such change. As regards drainage I am not sure there was not an element of wisdom in their opposition. Up-to-date schemes and modern appliances are all very well in towns, but in remote country districts there are few to understand them and handle them efficiently. In like manner I have seen most beautiful organs presented to country churches, where there has been no one to play them decently.

And by contrast those who dubbed themselves Tories or Conservatives were the party of reform and progress in our countryside life, and could always be relied upon to help.

One morning I was told a woman wished to see me. Before she spoke, I judged her age to be about seventy. Her face was wrinkled and her hair quite white. "I am afraid father is ailing and mother is not too well either. I shall be glad if you will come and see them some day soon," was her request.

"Your father and mother?" I involuntarily exclaimed in some surprise. "Yes," she shortly replied. "Can't I have a father and a mother?" I apologised for my apparent rudeness, and asked their ages. Her mother, she said, was ninety, and her father ninety-three.

The next day I went to the lonely farmhouse situated near the end of a far-off ghyll. I knocked at the door once or twice and, getting no response, entered the dimly lighted kitchen. I saw seated on one side of the fire a very old woman with snow-white hair, and apparently quite blind. As soon as she heard me, she began to grope for her wooden briar pipe, which had fallen on the ground. She would have nothing to say to me till I had recovered it and given her a light, when, after a few decided draws, she pointed with her thumb to the ceiling. "It's John," she said, "and he's uncommon bad."

So I went upstairs to see John. He was lying on his back, peacefully sleeping his way to the greater world beyond. His pulse could still be felt, but he was unconscious. I carefully turned him on one side—a golden rule when dealing with the dying. It was a simultaneous and natural decay of every organ.

I then leisurely examined the beautiful old brown oak furniture of the bedroom, all well-polished with a hundred years of beeswax and elbow grease. In fact every article of furniture in that old moorland farmhouse was good solid brown oak. What rare bargains could be picked up in those days in these far-off dales, before the ubiquitous curio-dealer began to poke about on his cycle or motor cycle. At the sale shortly afterwards, I bought a delft rack for 10s., now worth £12, and a lovely old dresser for £2, 10s., now worth at least £50.

I then returned to talk to the old lady. "Well," she said, "what do you think to John?" "John," I replied, "is very bad—in fact dying." "Ye never says so," she exclaimed in great surprise. "Well," she added, "I knew it would come to this, and warned him times without end to take care of himself. But he would never heed. He's been that man for rampaging and clashing about, that he's mashed himself up and fair ruined his constitution."

Good gracious, I reflected, what a land for a doctor to settle in! They ruin their constitutions yet live to be ninety-three.

There was some truth and justice in the old lady's plaint after all, as I found out afterwards.

It appears that John had been a cattle drover in the long past years when there were no railways. His journeys had taken him far afield—to Westmoreland, Cumberland, and Scotland. He had been very quarrelsome, a heavy drinker, and briefly was what they call in the Yorkshire dales "a miraklous man." He had made some bitter enemies, and these had once waylaid and so brutally handled him, that they left him for dead on the open moor. He lay there two whole days and then managed to crawl home. Though recovery was thought to be impossible, he lived through it all, and began sheep farming.

Then his dutiful and faithful wife began to nag at him to take care of himself, and she went on nagging for fifty long years, till the end came at last.

Many of these moorland farmhouses have most picturesquely furnished kitchens, the mere sight *of* which is worth a long journey. The picture is before me now—the dresser with its blue willow-pattern plates and dishes and pewter vessels, the long settle, the oak kist, the oak eight-day clock, the many coloured samplers, the knife-box, and the brass warming pan; the hams and the sides of bacon hanging from the roof; the sheep-dogs on the floor, and the peat fire.

Should you be invited to taste the ham and hear some of the moorland stories, you may count yourself a fortunate man.

During a plague of influenza I was attending an old patriarch of ninety-four. The curious feature about this old man was his extraordinarily deep and gruff voice. I wondered he had the strength to produce such a huge volume of sound. I have rarely heard anything like it from normal lungs, but from ninety-four-year-old lungs it was ordinary phenomenal. The prognosis in his case was naturally a grave one, but to our astonishment he recovered. During his recovery he was very talkative. One day after receiving my congratulations on his marvellous constitution, he remarked, " I ruined my constitution by lying out a day and a night in a snowdrift in that snowstorm."

"What snowstorm?" I asked. "Why," he replied, "that big snowstorm of course." We had had a terrible snowstorm some seven years before, and I naturally thought he was alluding to this. I remarked that I had been out in it.

"Were you in it too?" he asked in much surprise. "Yes," I said, "up to the neck." We compared notes, and it gradually dawned on me that we were possibly talking about different storms. To make sure of the point I asked again, "You mean the great storm seven years ago?" "No," he bellowed. " Nowt ot soart, I mean t'big storm in 1831. I tell ee I ruined my constitution in it."

A few days afterwards he said, "It'll be a hanging job arter all for me afore ye're right shut on me."

At six o'clock one dark winter's morning I was roused by a very loud knocking at the door. On my opening it a few minutes afterwards, a tall gaunt old man strode quickly past me into my kitchen, whither I followed him. Fiercely addressing me he said, "Do you lig (lie) in bed all day here?" "No," I protested. Taking off his cap and pointing to some large wens on his head, he commanded, "Cut those damned things off, and if you can't cut 'em off, cut my damned old head off." I inquired this old ruffian's age (because he looked old). "Ninety last May," he answered.

Tackling seven wens in an old man of ninety, with no hot water or fire, on a cold winter's morning, was rather a tall order, so I temporised. I suggested that in such cold weather he might get erysipelas or cold in the wounds. "There's summat i' that," he replied. "I'll come when it is warmer, good morning," and marched off again. Country people have a dread of getting what they call "cauld" in the wounds.

I had forgotten all about him, when one summer morning at five o'clock there was another loud knock at my front door. Putting my head through the open window I saw my friend again. "Do you lig in bed all day here?" was again his salutation. On this occasion there was nothing to be done but tackle the job.

After closely watching my preparations, he remarked characteristically, "It strikes me there's going to be a bloody mess. I think we ought to be in the stable."

I removed the seven wens without his turning a hair or showing the slightest sign of pain. He asked the "damages," and on my naming the fee there ensued a hard Yorkshire bargaining. He beat me down unmercifully, and I got much the worst of it. Then I mentioned the necessary dressings. "Dressings! Dressings!" he said, "What's them? I've never heard of such things."

I told him the stitches would have to come out. "We'll see about that when t'time comes," he replied as he strode away.

I met him about a month afterwards, and so tough was the old moorcock that all had gone on well without dressings.

He was quite a man of substance, and had been a marvellously successful poacher. One of his farms, he told me, had been bought entirely from the proceeds of his poaching depredations. No one, it was said, could call a hare or a grouse so cleverly as he in the whole district.

There was the greatest difficulty in persuading these old people to lie in bed. They were not used to it. Moreover, they regarded it as a reminder that even they were mortal. When they had been in bed a few days they used to say they had "Thowt a lot." This is a well-understood Yorkshire formula, meaning contemplation of the latter end. They tried to compromise by offering to stay in the "house," which in Yorkshire always denotes the kitchen, usually the living-room of the farm.

I was one day strongly urging an old man of eighty-eight, who was known throughout the district as "T'aud Lad," and was as obstinate as his namesake, to stay in bed for a few days. At last he consented, though very reluctantly, and when I left him I felt quite pleased with my success.

Unfortunately a few minutes afterwards I met the parson who inquired who were on the sick list. I mentioned T'aud Lad among the others.

A few days afterwards I had a very stormy

reception from T'aud Lad. Instead of being in bed, he was in the "house" with boots, hat, coat, and walking-stick ready for an expedition abroad. "You gave me up," he shouted angrily. "No," I protested in the negative. "Oh yes, you did. You told me to lig in bed, and then you sent t'parson. I'll show ee whether I'm going to dee or not. I'm going out for a walk." This the obstinate old man at once proceeded to do, and lived some years afterwards.

Edward Metcalfe, a retired Yorkshire sheep-farmer, aged ninety-two, recognised that his time had at last come, turned his face to the wall, and prepared to depart in peace.

The vicar of the parish in which Metcalfe, or Mecca, as he was called, lived, was one of the kindest, most earnest and exemplary parsons I have ever met in a long experience.

Unfortunately he suffered from a chronic minor ailment of the nose, dry catarrh, which caused him no little inconvenience.

As soon as the vicar heard that Mecca was numbered among the sick, he hurried to his bed-side. It happened to be a very healthy time, and as there was no one else ill he concentrated all his zeal on the dying man. He visited him two or three times a day, reading to him, exhorting him, and praying for him.

At first the old man was very much pleased with these attentions but, as death lingered, he began to weary of them, and to wish to be left alone to die in peace.

Late one evening the vicar, who had been if possible more earnest than usual in his ministration, leaned over the dying man and said, "Good-night, my dear brother, I shall come and see you first thing in the morning."

Suddenly, by a great effort Mecca sat up "on end" and said, "I'll tell ye what it is, Vicar."

"Yes," replied the vicar, earnestly listening.

"I tell ye what it is, Vicar," gasped Mecca.

"Yes! Yes!" said the vicar, thinking it was a dying confession and trying not to miss a word. "Speak up!"

"Y're breeath's noan so varra sweeat I can tell ye."

Another story I must relate in passing of this faithful priest. His only daughter, to whom he was devotedly attached, was very dangerously ill, and her recovery considered very doubtful. At the crisis, when life was in the balance, her father who, though a holy and devout man, found it almost impossible to reconcile himself to his possible loss, wandered restlessly in and out of the houses of his parishioners, seeking the sympathy they were willing enough to give.

One of these, after kindly inquiry said, "Well, parson, I'se thankful to say ye're not alone in your trubble."

"Oh!" asked the parson in quick sympathy. "Are you in trouble too?"

"Ah is an' all. I'se sadly trubbled, I can tell ee," replied the farmer.

"Oh do tell me what it is and let me share it, and then let us kneel down together," begged the parson.

"I'se sadly trubbled. T'aud sow is varra bad, and t'missis an' I we've bin up all neight doctoring 'er," was the farmer's explanation.

"Good gracious me, don't compare my darling to a pig," shouted the distracted parson as he rushed out of the house.

The farmer's sympathy was very real. The sow was a prolific one and helped to pay the rent. Moreover, anybody who has ever had any veterinary experience, knows quite well that of all domestic animals the pig is by far the most difficult and hopeless to treat.

I was once called in by a farmer who, with the friendly aid of his neighbours, was busily engaged in doctoring a sick pig. He slung the animal up by a rope and proceeded to pour so much neat gin down its throat that it expired on the spot.

The parson's daughter recovered but the farmer's pig died.

When I suddenly left the moorlands through illness, a message was received by my successor summoning him to see an old man of ninety-four. It was not that he was specially ailing, but he might suddenly "slip away" or "pop off" without being seen by a doctor, which would have been very awkward for the relations. I knew the man well as a fierce, quarrelsome old fellow. His daughter, seeing a stranger, hesitated for some time about allowing him to see the old Tartar. She saw the possibility of a paragraph in the *Darlington Times* headed "Sensational Murder of a Moorland Doctor," and explained her fears. My successor, who was like myself over six feet, thought he could surely take care of himself in a struggle with an old man of ninety-four, and went upstairs. He described the scene very graphically to me. A tall, gaunt, old giant was sitting nearly naked on the edge of the bed. He looked up, and as it slowly dawned on his old brain that it was a stranger and not his old doctor, his face gradually assumed a fierce tigerish expression and he began clawing the air with his bony fingers. There was a long pause during which my friend thought he was preparing to spring at his throat; then hissing like a serpent he spat out, "Ah'll noan tak yer bloody mooky stooff."

The moorlanders had more than the usual horror of an inquest, and as for a *post-mortem* examination, it was really a terrible blot on the family escutcheon, never to be wiped out. One day, in conversation with a farmer, I referred to an unfortunate suicide which had occurred on the moors. "What could ye expect?" was his natural comment. "Ye know, his faither war oppened."

About the Author

About the Author
by someone who knew him

READERS of this book who have become interested in the personality
of its author may welcome a short account of his life.

R. W. S. Bishop spent his youth at Ripon ; entered as a medical
student at Leeds (it was before the days of the University), and
after some two or three years there went to London and studied
at St Mary's Hospital, whence he qualified as M.R.C.S. and L.R.C.P.
in 1889.

He then went to Paris, where he studied in the hospitals under
Charcot and other famous French teachers. It was at this time
that he acquired the love for and fluency in the use of the French
language which remained with him to the very last, so that in
his dying hours he spoke almost as much French as English.

On returning to England he spent some years as assistant to
doctors practising in the neighbourhood of Sheffield, and among
the Derbyshire hills before settling at Bradford as House-Surgeon
to the Children's Hospital.

But he was by nature no townsman, and finally the call of the
moorlands was not to be resisted. He was not only a notable
angler, but had a real and deep feeling for wild country and for
unsophisticated country people.

Of his prowess with the rod and his love of nature, a contributor
to the *Yorkshire Post* writes :—"Dr Bishop was widely known in
the North, especially to anglers, and his wonderful gift of memory
made him ever welcome on a dull day. He was a member of the
Yorkshire Fishery Board, the Yorkshire Esk Fishery, and the
Yorkshire Angling Associations ; also of the Tanfield Angling Club
(of which he was Hon. Secretary for many years), and in his earlier
days of several other fishing associations. . . . Many a salmon—
in one year thirty-eight—paid the penalty of attraction to his fly
on his best-known river, and the trout and the grayling had no

BIOGRAPHICAL NOTE

deadlier tempter than he, both there and in the smaller streams to which he had welcome access. Being greatly interested in the free passage of salmon up the rivers, he erected a salmon pass at his own expense at Newby. Birds had in him a firm friend and protector; even the heron, with its predilection for salmon and trout fry, was not banned."

In 1894 he acquired a practice at Kirkby Malzeard (on the edge of the moor north of Ripon), where he worked for twelve years. It was during these years that most of the material of his book was stored in his really remarkable memory. When asked during his last illness whether he had not any notes to assist his writing, he replied, tapping his forehead with a long finger, "Only there."

"As a physician," writes the friend who furnishes these notes, "he was characterised by an extreme conscientiousness. He has told me how after walking home some miles late at night from a difficult case, he has gone to bed and, unable to sleep because of some idea that he had overlooked some point, he has got up and dressed again and trudged off through a winter night over miles of dark lanes back to the patient's house to satisfy himself on the point which he might have overlooked. I can fully credit it. It is just the sort of thing he *would* do. I have naturally met and sometimes attended a good many of his old patients and have been much struck with the powerful impression he had made on them. He understood them so well that he was able to make them do anything he recommended, and they had the most implicit faith in anything that Dr Bishop had said.

"Speaking from the professional point of view, I thought him a very discerning and thoughtful physician. His knowledge was up to date, and he read a good many recent books on medical subjects. Most remarkable was the way in which he gained the confidence of his patients of all classes. I always felt that he would have made a mark in a much wider and more prominent sphere if he had cared to do so. But he loved the country and country-folk, and would perhaps never have been happy in a town."

On retiring from practice Dr Bishop made his home in Tanfield on the River Ure. Here in 1915 he was attacked by a painful and, as it proved, fatal disease, whose progress the best treatment and the most devoted nursing failed to arrest. His book was written during the last year of his life, in the intervals of acute suffering. He died on 31st December 1921 and was buried in Tanfield Churchyard.

J. C. POWELL.

Index

Index

INDEX